The Early Years

by Mark Hodkinson

Queen

OMNIBUS PRESS

The Early Years

Queen

Copyright © 1995 Omnibus Press
(A Division of Book Sales Limited)

Edited by Chris Charlesworth & Johnny Rogan.
Cover & book designed by Michael Bell Design.
Picture research by Mark Hodkinson & Nicola Russell.

ISBN 0-7119-4820-8
Order No. OP47753

Exclusive Distributors:
Book Sales Limited
8/9 Frith Street, London W1V 5TZ, UK.
Music Sales Corporation
257 Park Avenue South, New York, NY 10010, USA.
Music Sales Pty Limited
120 Rothschild Avenue, Rosebery, NSW 2018, Australia.

To the Music Trade only:
Music Sales Limited
8/9 Frith Street, London W1V 5TZ, UK.

Front cover photograph: Redferns.
Back cover photograph: Barry Plummer.

Every effort has been made to trace the copyright holders
of the photographs in this book but one or two were unreachable.
We would be grateful if the photographers concerned
would contact us.

A catalogue record for this book is available from
the British Library.

Printed in the United Kingdom by
Redwood Books Limited, Trowbridge, Wiltshire.

Introduction

Queen

Once they've made it, rock stars and their narratives are pretty much all the same. They fall out acrimoniously with the people who got them there in the first place; date models, travel the world, become fabulously rich and take drugs; endure at least one grubby contractual dispute; meet lots of people but are routinely lonely. And then, if they don't die, split up, or crack up, they emerge as astute businessmen writing songs yearning for the guileless, witless, much less (of everything) days of before.

Queen were typical, if not the most typical rock group ever to exist. Their only singular feature, aside from sheer longevity and an unusual degree of consistency, was that their front man became the first famous rock star to die of Aids.

There is, however, in every story of fame, a before and after. The 'after' is the model thrown in the gigantic cake at the album launch party, and the sycophants and apologists for a life too hectic, too indulgent to even write a note home. We know this life well. Newspapers and magazines provide habitual bulletins of this extravagance and recklessness: he's sleeping with her, he's smashed up that hotel, she's snubbed so-and-so, he's sleeping with him. We know this life too well.

The 'before' life is far more fascinating. This is where we find the desperation and dedication, the indignity and indecision. This is where, of the first UK rock generation, Brian Jones is a bus conductor poncing around jazz clubs talking wearisomely of his new group, The Rollin' Stones; where, of Queen's peers, Elton John plays standards for a pound a night in a London pub; where, of the current rock protagonists, Morrissey, the renowned ascetic, pesters a friend of mine - two phone calls and a postcard - to feature an interview with his new band, The Smiths, in a 12-page photo-copied fanzine.

This is their secret life and it is the publicist's first duty to erase it, or at the very least relate it selectively. The official promotional biography usually begins with the first single, everything up until this point is deemed insignificant. The atrocious early gigs and the hilarious first publicity shots are spirited away, burned, and the ashes scattered on the moors.

Queen - The Early Years is an examination of those formative musical days in the lives of the four people who became Queen. Their childhood and family histories are dealt with concisely; they are entertainers, not politicians. Moreover, other people's childhoods, like other people's dreams, are often tedious. Instead, the book is a collection of anecdotes and thoughts of those who knew them mainly in the 'before' life, when they were real people - unsure, apprehensive, eager, imprudent, dogged - not yet the cartoons they became: Freddie the camp trouper; Roger the steadfast, soft-eyed rocker; Brian the match stick guru of the guitar; and John the stoic technician abashed by the spotlight.

It is a story which can be told relatively explicitly since it is not encumbered by vested interests. Its players have nothing to lose, unlike those that came afterwards who invested money, time, emotion and a career serving Queen. A standard biography on the group will only ever draw forth a percentage of these, and since the network around them, from the fan club to the management, is peculiarly solicitous, the unexpurgated account will either remain unwritten or suffer from the dishonour of compromise, much like the existing over-laundered official biography.

Here then are the early days of their lives, presented hopefully in the sanguine, ardent and enthusiastic fashion in which they were lived.

Mark Hodkinson, June 1995.

Acknowledgements

Paula Ridings for your encouragement, support, and love. My parents and grandmother for watching out for me. Chris Charlesworth for valued suggestions, corrections and deadline extension. Andrew King for believing in the project. Johnny Rogan, for Educating Hodkinson, and altruism all too rare in a selfish world.

And, finally, the following who shared a drink, telephone number, house space, book, video, advice, or secret: John Adams, John Baltitude, Peter Bartholomew, Neil Battersby, Peter Bawden, Ronnie Beck, Mike Bersin, Tony Brainsby, Roger Brokenshaw, Greg Brooks, Les Brown, Nigel Bullen, Clive Castledine, David Cooper, Kim Cooper, Trevor Cooper, Dave Dilloway, Michael Dudley, Chris Dummett, Tony Ellis, Rik Evans, Jeremy Gallop, Dorothy Gill-Carey, Gillian Green, Michael Grime, John Grose, Vaughan Hankins, Gill Hankins, Bob Harris, Jenny Hayes, Mike Heatley, Sean Hewitt, Geoff Higgins, Win Hitchens, Ed Howell, Rob Kerford, Fran Leslie, Sam Lind, Dave Lloyd, Paul Martin, John Matheson, Barry Mitchell, Geoff Moore, Barbara Morrison, Guy Patrick, Mark Paytress, Richard Penrose, Geoff Pester, Josephine Ranken, Phil Reed, Mark Reynolds, Bill Richards, Peter Rowan, John Sanger, Tim Staffell, Carol Stringer, John Stuart, John Taylor, William Telford, Ken Testi, Nathan Tiller, Richard Thompson, Helen Tonkin, Sarah Triptree, Joop Visser, Lawrence Webb, Rod Wheatley, Jane Wilderspin, Dave Williams, Andy Wright, Eileen Wright, Richard Young.

Clucksville

Chapter 1

Queen

Queen are everywhere, still; not quite the Coca Cola Company or Ford, but not too far behind. Freddie Mercury died in November 1991 and the group folded immediately afterwards, but the cliché is authentic and the legend really does live on. It endures because we live in the age of the rewind. Digital remastering, video technology, CDi, CD ROM – no one dies any more, bands no longer split up, the song goes on forever. We play them, pause them, hold them as our own at that moment we cherish the most. And, simultaneously, across town, where the housing estates wash up against the business parks, someone is dreaming of lunch time or home time as she packs the traditional Queen memorabilia into cardboard boxes. The records, videos, T-shirts, posters, badges, postcards, bedspreads, and sew-on patches are set for the lorries and markets. Queen and Freddie Mercury are as alive as they ever were.

We can, of course, bequeath to anyone we choose this virtual immortality. At the very least, we are each of us on a wedding video somewhere or have mumbled into a tape recorder. Thankfully, there is a natural selection of sorts. Cameras and cassettes are placed in front of all pop stars, but not to the same extent as Queen. In simple terms, they had the songs and knew how to present them, in the studio and in concert. Their songs, from the Neanderthal pomposity of 'We Will Rock You' and 'Hammer To Fall' to the outlandish muse of 'Bohemian Rhapsody' and 'Killer Queen', were consumed voraciously by the public.

Between March 1974 and December 1992 Queen had forty-one UK Top 40 hits (one of them, 'Under Pressure', with David Bowie) and amassed nearly seven years' worth of Top 75 chart placings. Only one other group, Status Quo, have had more hits, and they had a six-year start on Queen. In fact, if the solo hit singles by members of Queen are added to their overall total, only three artists – Cliff Richard, Elvis Presley and Elton John – have had more UK hits. Queen, of course, also sold albums, more than 80 million at the last count, and rising.

They were, on the surface at least, an unlikely force to acquire such widespread adoration. Fronted by a vainglorious bisexual, their music was schizophrenic; at different times absurd, choral, linear, funky, far-out, inane, rocking, mawkish or pulsating. Critics, and few had much regard for Queen save for a grudging acknowledgement of Freddie's stagecraft, claimed Brian May knew just one guitar solo, while Roger Taylor and John Deacon were supposedly nothing more, and nothing less, than rock journeymen. And yet few groups, if any, have honed so many styles of music into gilded hit singles. Their very appeal lay in their sheer size, and the other world – all glitzy and glamorous – stage side of the footlights. They were juggernaut rock incarnate, too bulky and brazen to embody any substantial cultural worth, but unsurpassed as entertainment value. When Freddie clenched his fist and Roger Taylor pounded the snare, Monday morning, the rain, the queue at the bus stop, the electricity bill, the smell of the office or the workshop, they were gone.

The Queen story routinely begins with Freddie Mercury and the tang of the exotic, of Zanzibar and the boy from the sun, the dusty street bazaars, the saffron curtains and drapes across the doorways of whitewashed buildings, a starched colonialist tradition; a most distinct upbringing. Of course, much of what made Freddie also defined Queen; without him they were merely a model rock band with a bent for a commercial tune, but like most stories of remarkable success, the prosaic qualities of graft, reliability, loyalty and organisation were the cardinal elements. These were largely Made in England, in Leicestershire, Cornwall, and Middlesex to be specific.

"John who?"

The courteous lady sitting at her desk in Oadby Library is eager to please.

"Was that Dea-kin or Dea-con?"

She can't help, but thinks she knows a person who can, possibly. She calls the main library in Leicester: they have some books there on Queen, gracious smile. She passes over a leaflet too, for the Leicestershire Record Office. On its cover is a photograph of a bearded man holding a magnifying glass. They have some newspaper cuttings there which might be of use, another gracious smile.

Oadby is six miles south of Leicester, the last real conurbation before the flat, sodden plains of green around the belly of England. Crows bicker in damp churchyards, villages have quaint names like Great Glen and Smeeton Westerby, and tomorrow will probably be much like today.

The library is a sunny building situated behind The Parade on the main road winding through the centre of Oadby, past Threshers, Woolworths, Boots and the Old Manor Inn where fine ales have been served for more than 300 years. The library was opened on 1 November 1969 by John Peel, not the DJ who gave Queen their first radio session, but the MP who represented the town in Parliament at that time. Its staff have heard of Queen, but not John Deacon. In its files only two famous sons of Oadby are commemorated, both of them felons, George Davenport, a highwayman, and James Hawker, a poacher. Quite clearly, John Deacon does not have enough colour or verve to pass muster and make the town's annals. Eventually, a solitary one-line mention of John is found. This fabulously wealthy, internationally famous musician has his name on a tiny index card housed in a wooden drawer in the local studies section. The cards cross-reference to newspaper clippings. Even here, poor John is allowed no rightful station. 'Deacon, John – rock musician, April 1974,' is placed between 'Daynight Electrical Contractors, Trade Boost, 25.2.74' and 'Deane, David, Marriage to Pauline Valerie Smith, 15.3.62.'

John Richard Deacon was born on August 19, 1951 at St Francis' Private Hospital, London Road, Leicester to Arthur Henry Deacon and Lillian Molly Deacon. The family lived at first in the Leicester suburb of Evington where John attended Lindon Junior School. Oadby, fast becoming a dormitory town for Leicester, was expanding rapidly in the Fifties, with an extensive network of new redbrick houses seeping over the countryside. Arthur Deacon had a certain amount of security with his job at the Norwich Union in Leicester so, in 1960 John and his younger sister of five years, Julie, moved with their parents to a detached house in Hidcote Road, Oadby. The road is on the edge of a large estate where cul-de-sacs and crescents are packed snugly into the available space. The properties are all strikingly similar, only the names of the streets change – Ash Tree Road, Brambling Way, Pine Tree Close, Rosemead Drive, rustic names for a rather monotonous suburbia.

After a short time at Langmoor Junior School in Oadby, John attended Gartree High School and Beauchamp [pronounced Beecham] Grammar School, both of them situated on the same site, just a few minutes walk away from Hidcote Road.

During his time in Oadby John Deacon wasn't so much quiet, as not really there, more a ghost of a boy. There was, of course, a physical outline, but even this was magnificently ordinary: short hair, briefcase, shirt tucked in the trousers, shiny shoes, a courteous 'Hello' or nod of the head as he passed. He read electronics magazines and built gadgets out of transistors; fished with his dad on the canal; did his homework; collected locomotive numbers; tried to please his parents, and no one noticed him very much.

"I don't remember him doing anything, what a boring character! There's no point in pretending he was anything else because he wasn't. I mean, he always seemed very nice, but he was just a bit quiet. I don't have any remarkable memories of him," says Jenny Hayes (née Fewins), exasperated, unable to summon a single anecdote about John Deacon after an hour's thought. And Jenny should know some, she was part of the gang which spawned John Deacon's first musical venture, The Opposition. For a short period of time, two or three shows at most, she was also the group's go-go dancer with her friend, Charmiane Cowper.

"The clearest memory I have of him is being in a dressing room and everybody getting changed after the show and larking about. John never said a word. He never said anything, never spoke. Ever so strange. He just got on with it, did it, but you're talking about a completely unremarkable character," said Jenny.

The Opposition fell together in the summer of 1965, before John had turned fourteen; this young age may explain his formal, remote manner at the time. They decided on the name simply because it was easy to remember. They were one of about four groups thriving in each school year at Beauchamp Grammar School. Leicester, like the rest of England, was clearly swinging. Fired by the chipper coffee bar pop of Herman's Hermits, Peter and Gordon, The Hollies, The Rockin' Berries, and, of course, The Beatles and The Rolling Stones, every teenager in the country had a guitar. Most strummed it a few times and then left it in the spare room, unable to fathom the re-tuning. Some, like the four members of The Opposition, saw it as an extension of their friendships and began to practise regularly.

John Deacon, or 'Deaks' as he was universally known, would seem an unlikely band member when he teamed up with his best friend from nearby Rosemead Drive, Nigel Bullen (drums), along with Richard Young (vocals/lead guitar) and Clive

Castledine (bass). "John was quite keen," said Clive Castledine. "I was amazed with his academic background that he stuck with music. He was extremely intelligent and worked very hard at school. I think he took to learning the guitar in possibly the same way he looked at education. He was keen and did it properly."

John had been strumming the acoustic guitar he bought with his early morning paper round wages since the age of twelve, firstly with a school pal, Roger Ogden, with whom he'd play along to records. He was already proficient when The Opposition began scratching out covers of The Yardbirds, The Animals and Tamla Motown classics. Richard Young was the driving force behind the group; rehearsals were held at his parents' and since he was from a fairly wealthy background (his dad owned an electrical wholesaling business) he loaned the others money to buy equipment. From the start they each had quality gear: John's guitar cost £60 which he promised to pay back to Richard on a weekly basis. Richard had no qualms about lending the others money, especially John, since he knew John's mother would never consider buying him one; she would have seen it as an impediment to his studies.

The group was infused with a warm camaraderie. They took a bus ride to Leicester together and brought back pieces of Nigel's kit on the bus and Richard cycled home from Cox's music store in King Street with a Vox AC30 amp on the handlebars, unlikely as it may seem. They played for friends at a party at Clive Castledine's house in September 1965 and at a dance at Gartree High School soon afterwards. Their first authentic public performance was at the Co-operative Hall in Enderby in December 1965. They soon became regulars at youth clubs in the villages dotted around Oadby. Their image was clean-cut, usually running to ties and suits. "We weren't cool or weird or anything, it was before those sort of days," said Clive. "We had really short hair, it was well before everyone went hairy and weird."

Unfortunately, after barely ten months in tenure, it was apparent that Clive's musicianship was trailing the others, all of whom were surprisingly adept for their ages. "I was the least proficient, to put it mildly," he recalls. "They had to bang the bass playing into my head. My heart wasn't in it and I wasn't giving it my best by a long chalk. I was getting outside interests called girls and bikes." Richard Young would coach Clive painstakingly through his parts, only for him to forget them on stage and drift out of key. "We all had a good idea about music except for Clive," says Richard. "He was a great chap but he had no idea at all. I once spent about two hours teaching him one song but he'd just play any old thing on stage. We had to sack him at the end." Unbeknown to anyone at the time, Clive's inept bass playing was a catalyst in John Deacon's journey to Queen. John had hitherto considered himself a guitarist, but magnanimously switched to bass to answer The Opposition's call. The moment was recorded in vivid detail in the band diary, fastidiously kept by Richard. The entry for April 2, 1966, reads: "We threw Clive out and had a practice in Deaks' kitchen with Deaks on bass – played much better."

The Opposition had been encouraged to dispense with Clive by Peter 'Pedro' Bartholomew, the singer with another local band, The Rapids Rave. The extrovert front man had been guest on one or two songs when the two bands were on the same bill, but his days with his own group were numbered. His dad had ordered him to leave The Rapids Rave because their busy schedule was affecting his engineering apprenticeship. Peter saw The Opposition, with their somewhat lower profile, as an ideal alternative, and they were keen for him to join. As Peter explains: "I said, 'Yes, I'll join you, on one understanding: you're all very talented, but your bass player's crap.' He just wasn't very musical. Clive really looked the part though, he was a good looking lad, but he just couldn't play. I told them they were a great little band but the bass player was spoiling it."

Clive, known within the circle of friends as 'Cluck', had, in fact, looked the part more than any of the others. He was one of the first in Oadby to own a Vespa scooter and properly embrace mod culture. It was, of course, a diluted version of the one colouring the streets of London but, all the same, skirts were getting higher, suits sharper and bellies were filling with attitude. "I was buying and selling scooters from home," said Clive. "Obviously the environment of Oadby was quite affluent so we were mainly mods. We weren't extreme at all. The background we all had was quite sheltered, we were brought up in a decent way with a good lifestyle. We'd have run a mile if we saw any rockers."

Peter Bartholomew lays claim to being the person who first suggested John Deacon should take over on bass. The group resorted to subterfuge for their first practice at Oadby Boys' Club featuring John on bass and Peter on vocals. Without informing Clive, they arranged to meet early so John could borrow Clive's equipment and run through a few songs. At the time the band was 'managed' by Anthony Hudson, an acquaintance who adopted the title of manager though no one could remember him ever earning it. "Anthony stood at the door of the club with his foot jammed in it," said Peter Bartholomew. "He was on the look-out for Clive and was going to signal to us if he saw him coming. John Deacon was brilliant on the bass straight away, he really took to it."

After a failed attempt to appease his parents by training as an accountant, Clive went on to make a career out of his hobby. Castledine Scooters became Clive Castledine Motorcycles, the main Honda and Suzuki dealer in Leicester, with a workshop and saleroom on the busy, shuddering dual carriageway of Humberstone Road. During the busy summer period he will sell ten bikes a week, and he is already planning to pass the business on to his son. In the shadow of two ugly tower blocks, surrounded by cans of Swarfega, oily rags, zips waiting to be stitched into motorcycle suits, and rows of burnished bikes, he has never coveted the lifestyle of his former musical colleague. "It has never gone through my mind to wish I'd followed the musical route," he points out. "It seems so long ago, almost insignificant really. I nearly gave music another go during the punk era. I liked the rawness of bands like The Stranglers and Sham 69, but I was working 60 hours a week on my business. I wouldn't know which way up to hold a bass guitar now."

Without Clive the band were able to develop at their own pace and there was no shortage of bookings. Leicester, like the rest of the country, was teeming with venues, from church halls to working men's clubs to theatres, and for the first time the UK had an infrastructure to support live music made by young people. Pop was also on television on its own terms, rather than as an addendum to light entertainment programmes, and everyone read the *Melody Maker*.

Although, like every other group, they harboured covert ambitions, The Opposition were largely content to learn their craft, become one of the best bands in Leicester, and then trust to the future. They appeared almost every Saturday night at the Co-op Hall in Enderby. They received a fee of £4 for their performance at the Co-op Hall, though by the end of 1966, when they were playing venues like Market Harborough Working Men's Club and Leicester Tennis Club, the fee had risen to £12.

Many of the shows were as support to Peter's former group, The Rapids Rave, whose membership comprised slightly older lads managed by Les Taylor. Eventually Les, whose stepson Robert Prince played lead guitar in The Rapids, also became manager of The Opposition. "I wanted to keep an eye on Robert," Les recalls. "They were playing in some rough places and I thought if I was manager at least I could keep a watch on what he was up to. The Opposition were just their back-up group, I didn't know them very well at all." Les often sold both groups as a package to venues, but his interest was always primarily in the well-being of his stepson, 'the Eric Clapton of the Midlands' as he refers to him. He remembers John Deacon as 'a lovely kid' but it was only decades later when he learned of John's phenomenal success. "I never had any ambitions in the music business," he says. "I just wanted to stop Robert falling into bad company. I used to just get them a few bookings here and there, it was easy in those days."

David Williams, another school friend, joined on lead guitar in July 1966 and Richard Young moved to his first love, keyboards. Appropriately, they added covers by The Zombies and The Spencer Davis Group. They made random attempts to write their own material, but a few instrumentals in the mode of Booker T and The MGs was the limit of their success.

When he first heard The Opposition, Dave Williams was unimpressed. He had already played in local bands The Glen Sounds and The Outer Limits and knew some of the elementary factors of life in a group, like tuning. "I went to a rehearsal and they sounded awful, like they hadn't tuned up," he recalls. "They had tuned up, but only to their own instrument, so they were all out of tune with each other. I advised them to get a pitch pipe and after that they didn't sound too bad."

John Deacon was a dedicated group member, anxious that the songs were arranged and performed properly, his perfectionism was already evident to the others. He was also, along with Richard, the group's archivist, collecting every newspaper cutting, even the tiny adverts for shows published in the *Leicester Mercury*.

Molly Deacon still considered the group a frivolous aside in her son's life. Her husband had died in 1962 when John was just ten and she was determined to hold some discipline over him, especially in directing him towards an academic career. In September 1966 the band had been booked to play the Tudor Rose pub in Atherstone and, wary of Molly's strictness, they coaxed John out of the house and into the garden while they related the details. Unfortunately the kitchen window was open and she overheard. "She came storming out saying,'John's not playing in any pubs', and that was it," said Nigel Bullen. "We had to get a stand-in for the night. He was only about sixteen at the time and under age, but that's just the way she was, a bit strict."

A small club scene developed in Leicester and The Opposition were part of it, appearing regularly at Granny's and The Casino in London Road, on the same circuit boasting gloriously unknown bands like Strictly For The Birds, The Executives, Sweetheart, Cedar Set and Wellington Kitch. The Night Owl was perhaps the most hip club. Geno Washington appeared there and the all-nighters were said to attract hipsters from as far afield as London. Much of it was a parody of the scene in the capital, but at the time Paris, New York, and the whole world was two strides (in zip-up, knee length plastic boots) behind London anyway.

Earnest rather than intense, The Opposition were still far from provincial clods. David Williams, who quickly became their MC as well as guitarist, brought with him more than an essence of style, refulgent in make-up and bearing the nickname 'Pussy' after the television glove puppet, Pussy Cat Willum. He was later to attend Loughborough Art College, but in the meantime his artistic bent led to some experimentation with drugs, mainly dope but a 'little bit of acid'; his home-made cakes were always popular at parties. If it was OK for The Beatles... was Dave's doctrine. The band, anxious to cultivate an image, began to wear silk shirts, each member in a different colour.

They might have appeared unerringly normal, but they were actually characters in their own right. Richard Young ("He was so straight, he was weird" – Dave Williams) was known for the odd touch of eccentricity. He would over-tune his car so it ran fast, so fast that it would move without anyone touching the accelerator. He would park it, leave the engine running, pretend to close the door, and then run alongside it in fake panic as if it was driving itself away. Another routine was reserved for the chemist's shop. He would burst in clutching his throat, frothing at the mouth, imploring the assistant to "Get me my pills, quick."

The Who were a prevailing influence on The Opposition and eventually even John Deacon had the regulation scooter, a Vespa 180. "We all had the parkas and everything," said Dave Williams. "I remember there was a ford at the bottom of our road and John was coming round to my house one evening. He skidded and came off the scooter. There was quite a lot of blood and he was pretty stressed out when he got to our place, in fact, it's about the only time I ever saw John stressed out!"

London had wanton go-go girls in cages decorating trendy clubs where kids smoked French cigarettes and wore sunglasses, forever waiting for the film crew to arrive. The Opposition had two giggling school friends who, tired of watching but not joining in, volunteered their services. Jenny Fewins and Charmiane Cowper had the nerve, if not the candid sexuality or polish; all the same, sometime in 1967, they became the band's go-go girls, and Dave Williams was quite appreciative: "I thought they were quite sexy, they had bosoms before most girls." Their routine was completely improvised. "We used to get up on stage and do this very, very simplistic dance. It was frightening really, especially when you realised we should have worked it all out a bit before we got up there, but most things weren't planned in the Sixties," said Jenny.

It was still a worthwhile experience for Jenny. On her seventeenth birthday her mother paid for an intensive modelling course and it led to three years' work via the Kathy Parker Agency in Leicester. Her good looks (listed as follows in her modelling brochure: Height: 5' 5", Bust: 36", Waist: 25", Hips: 36", Shoes 4 - 4 1/2) and trained poise helped sell packets of Player's cigarettes among other products. She also appeared at parades in seaside towns, usually to open summer seasons by celebrities.

Peter Bartholomew was the outsider in the group, not really a member of their clique; he was three years older and quite single-minded. He told them he could secure more bookings than Anthony Hudson who had now adopted the name of Anto Hudson to reflect his status in the pop business. Anto soon went the same way as Clive 'Cluck' Castledine, or, as the lads preferred, he went Clucksville.

Peter wanted the group to go up market, to shop at Leicester's premier music emporium, Moore and Stanworth's in Belgrave Road, rather than at Cox's where the guitars hung by their tuning pegs and flapped against the wall every time someone walked through the front door. He took John Deacon to buy an Ampeg amplifier for his bass; it sounded fine but, more importantly, it had a luminous green glow in the dark.

Some of Peter Bartholomew's designs were rejected and, eventually, his paternal concern was perhaps his downfall. "I was working at a shop at the time called Irish Linen which sold really trendy stuff," he explains. "I made them all come in and kitted them out in polo neck shirts. John Deacon did not like it at all. He said, 'We look like a load of poofs, I want to wear what I want to wear.' I was a bit surprised by this. I was supposed to be the older, wiser person who knew, but he just said, 'No way!'"

In November 1967, after eight months in the group, Peter Bartholomew left The Opposition, though there were differing accounts of his exit. "Pedro showed off. I felt ashamed! Told him that he was leaving," was the terse entry in Richard Young's diary after a performance he considered too effusive for The Opposition. "I have always been flamboyant," conceded Peter. "I like to have a laugh and I was a bit daft. I said daft things. I thought it was absolutely brilliant when we put flash guns under Richard's organ and things like that." Peter's version had him being tempted away to join his brother's band, The Rivals, a group with a busier social diary and a greater rhythm'n'blues edge. He did return briefly to The Opposition, however, when he had a three-month stint on saxophone a year or two later.

Peter Bartholomew drifted out of groups, working as a milkman and on motorway construction before forming his own business installing telephone systems. He sold the firm to a French company and is now self-employed again in the same business, proud of a full order book. He still has an organ and guitar and sings in karaokes when he's out with friends, but has no regrets about leaving the music business behind. "When I see a band, a good band, performing in a pub I sometimes get the itch again, but when I see them afterwards loading up the van in the cold on the car park, I'm glad I'm out of it. I couldn't be more happier with my life than I am now, couldn't enjoy it more."

He became a Queen fan, though it was some time before he realised his former musical colleague was a member: "I was such a fan of Queen and I never recognised him. I used to sit there night after night listening to the albums." It was only when John Deacon reverted to his original short haircut that Peter realised: "We were watching television. I think he was on *Top Of The Pops* or something. I said to my wife, 'Look who that is, it's John Deacon.' She said, 'So?', and I said, 'No, it's *the* John Deacon, from Oadby, from The Opposition...' 'Oh my God!' she said,'." After the initial shock, Peter realised he wasn't surprised by John's success: "He was the most talented in The Opposition, it was as if he had been born with a bass in his hand. He was always brilliant. He really deserved to get on. He was so relaxed when he played, always so confident."

Another member was Richard Frew who lasted just a month on guitar, before being replaced by the dextrous Ronald Chester. Ronald was an integral member, helping Richard Young with the band administration. For a month or two they were fronted by a singer called Carl, whose surname they forgot to log, but he left early in 1967. Whatever the line-up, The Opposition formed a merry crew as they drove through the hedge-flanked lanes of Leicestershire to another performance; arguments were rare and they had an unusual rapport. Sometimes the van would break down, venues would double book, amplifiers would explode, the band would bicker, someone would forget an effects pedal, the set list would change three songs in; this was John Deacon's musical apprenticeship and it was extraordinarily thorough.

Word got round that there was another band called The Opposition, so Oadby's Opposition became The New Opposition in April 1966, but then changed back again in January 1967. A few months later, on another whim, they became The Art, because, according to Richard Young, "Dave Williams was arty." They were all extremely young, so even by the summer of 1969 when John Deacon finally left, he was still a few months from his eighteenth birthday.

John Deacon played his final concert with The Art at Great Glen Youth and Sports Centre in August 1969, his place being taken immediately by another local musician, John Savage. John had been accepted on a course to study electronics at Chelsea College, an affiliate of London University. He had been with the group for four years, during which time they had played an average of one show each week. While it was invaluable experience in the grist of life in a pop group, it was irrefutably a small town enterprise. Two of their typically homespun comical episodes are again related best in the staccato style of diarist Richard: '26 September 1966 – Blackbird Motors Annual Dance, very dusty from the straw bales,' and 15 October 1966: 'Suddenly Deaks had pains in his stomach and had to play near the open window at the side of the stage for fear of being sick.'

For all the committed slog and sincere intent, four years after their début, The Opposition had not strayed more than a few miles from Leicester: they had no studio experience (though, just weeks after John left, they recorded an acetate of covers at Beck's studio in Wellingborough); no dealings with the music business aside from one or two local agents; and, perhaps most importantly, were not writing their own material. Their parochialism was epitomized by their decision, early in 1968, to buy a seven-year-old Morris van. A group with wider horizons would have used the money to fund a record pressing, or time in a studio, train fares to London to see potential managers, a poster campaign, or a complete re-location to the capital, but this wasn't The Opposition's style. "We wanted to be one of the best bands in Leicester, or around the locality," explains Richard. "I think I was under the misapprehension that the better you sounded and the more professional you got, you gradually went up the ladder, but it just doesn't work like that. It took me a long time to realise you could be a load of shit but if you got the right promotion you'd go far; that's what it is all about."

A new group came through in Leicester and The Opposition, especially Richard, were made decisively aware of the potency of promotion, style over content. In the space of just a few weeks a flash new group called Legay (named after the drummer's surname) were packing venues in the town; the same places at which The Opposition had appeared repeatedly, where they had diligently - but slowly - augmented their fan base. "Legay used to annoy Richard intensely," said Nigel Bullen. "They really had got the image. They were doing heavy rock versions of Tamla Motown and the places they played were packed with all the gorgeous women in Leicester. Musically they were very average." Unknown to the rest, John Deacon was already making salient mental notes. Legay, for their part, mutated into something far more routine; by 1970 they were Gypsy, stalwarts of the London pub circuit, eventually releasing two quietly received albums on United Artists.

Despite John's impending departure, Richard continued taking bookings for The Opposition. Some of these were out of town, in Southsea and Newcastle-upon-Tyne. A year after John's departure, however, Richard also left, to take up the position of pianist with Fearn's Brass Foundry. The soul covers band were appearing live five nights each week and had some of the finest musicians in Leicester; it was too much of a temptation to Richard who felt his own home-grown project had run its natural course. He drifted on to the cabaret circuit and stayed there for the next seventeen years. Music took him to many parts of the world when he became a performer on cruise ships, but he quit roaming in 1986 and set himself up in Leicester as a piano tuner and teacher.

The period during which John Deacon had been in The Opposition had seen profound changes in pop music. The Beatles and The Rolling Stones, to whom much of the decade's zeitgeist was subscribed, evolved from the radiant but callow pop of 'Help!' and 'Satisfaction' in the summer of 1965 to the ripened and urbane muse of 'Abbey Road' and 'Let It Bleed' just four summers later. Tommy Steele, Cliff Richard, Dusty Springfield et al invented the British teenager, but dressed it in similar clothes and the same benign attitude as its parents. By 1969 it had learned to be sullen, enigmatic, insolent, anything it wanted to be. The British brothers of the blues like Eric Clapton, Jimmy Page, Roger Daltrey, Ian Anderson, Keith Richards and Ray Davies had grown their hair, shredded the suits, and the din from the WEM speakers was no longer apologetic or restrained.

The Opposition had tried to assimilate this new energy – they used a fuzz box as early as October 1966, but they were decent lads from decent homes with 'A' Levels and college to work towards. John Deacon actually left Beauchamp with eight 'O' Levels and three 'A' Levels at grade A, a remarkable achievement considering his fairly heavy workload with the group. The Opposition had invigorated their set by judiciously adding covers by the likes of Jethro Tull and Deep Purple. In fact, Deep Purple were a seminal influence on John Deacon. On one of the last outings with his Leicester friends before he left for college, John, Richard and Nigel saw

Deep Purple at the Royal Albert Hall. They were already enthused by Deep Purple's 'Book Of Taliesyn' album and the concert in London was with a full orchestral backing, to be released a year later as 'Concerto For Group And Orchestra'. "It was an amazing night, a big influence on all of us," said Richard. "We were mesmerised by it, the orchestra, the playing, we really thought it was something very special. We talked about it in the car all the way back to Leicester."

Across The Tamar

Chapter II

It's the end of the night, a long night. The harsh fluorescent light backstage is a keen contrast to a few hours earlier when the faces before Roger Taylor melted into the darkness. He was on stage, back home in Truro, and the 800 people out there were merely shadows welded together. He could sense the attachment, he bathed in it in fact, but now the figures had broken free of the shadowy glue and were shaking his hand.

"Hello Roger, do you remember me? I knew you when..." He smiles courteously, laughs openly, he appears to have time for everyone. He's back at Truro City Hall promoting his first solo album since the demise of Queen. As he explained on stage, his career has gone full circle. He began at the City Hall nearly 30 years ago when his first serious group, Johnny Quale and The Reaction, competed in the town's 'rock and rhythm championship'.

Matt Vinyl, rock journalist for the *Cornish Guardian*, is straining to hear. By day, Matt Vinyl is Sean Hewitt the school teacher, but everyone in Cornwall has two jobs, if not two names. Matt, for it is he, not Sean, we find at such a rare rock 'n' roll evening in Truro, is listening in. He's at that comfortable distance, part of the décor, unobtrusive, and still able to hear every word, notice every gesture. There have been a few awkward moments as the carousel of Roger Taylor's past is spun before him – a school pal unrecognised, a clumsy handshake, a back accidentally turned on a former neighbour. Roger Taylor has dealt with it all skilfully; not 'professionally' since that would suggest a feigned bonhomie. There's a twinkle in his eyes, a warmth about his manner. It seems genuine, the real thing. Matt watches the last well-wisher gripping his hand for six seconds too long, asking him another banal question. It's at this point, as Roger Taylor turns to his people, the personal assistants on the pay roll, that Matt Vinyl expects to hear perhaps a touch of sarcasm, or arrogance, or detect a sense of relief that the ordeal is over. There is not a hint. "Right folks, shall we see where we can get a cup of tea in this place?" asks Roger Taylor. Matt Vinyl is impressed.

Cornish people tend to stay put, but Roger Taylor has travelled the globe, become a millionaire, had beautiful women as lovers, and more than likely bathed in champagne; but they staunchly believe he's remained 'one of them'. Their pride in him is palpable, they still talk about the time he clenched his fist in a victory salute at the end of *Juke Box Jury* and shouted: 'Up Truro'. When you're marooned on the in-step of England, and the number of people in your entire county is fewer than the inhabitants of nearby Plymouth, perhaps it pays to cherish your famous sons. And, make no mistake, Roger Taylor is cherished. If the fancy took him, per se, he could walk on water, maybe on one of the three rivers converging on the city, the Kenwyn, the Allen or the Truro itself.

Roger Taylor was actually born on the other side of England, in Kings Lynn, Norfolk, another town in quarantine, pressed up close to the sea on the east of England. He was born on July 26, 1949, at the West Norfolk and Kings Lynn Hospital, the son of Winifred and Michael Taylor, a civil servant working for the Ministry of Food. He was given the middle name of Meddows, a badge worn by members of his family through several generations. He attended Gaywood Primary School in Kings Lynn for three years before his father had to move with his job to Cornwall. The family, which now included Roger's sister, Clare, born in 1953, settled in Truro.

Truro is best known for its splendid cathedral, built at the end of the eighteenth century. It helps to draw in tourists who have become the town's lifeblood since the collapse of the tin mining industry and the port side trade. It claims, along with Bodmin, to be the 'capital' of Cornwall, a typically insular dogfight which matters deeply to people eager to maintain a gritty Cornish identity. They once had their own language and many place names are prefixed by 'Pol', 'Per' and 'Tre' from the original Gaelic vocabulary. Villages are knotted together by a web of quiet roads, across moors and downs, with outlandish names like Indian Queens, Gweek, Cripplesease, Twelveheads and Boconnoc. They want better roads to bring in the tourists and their jangling pockets, but, paradoxically, they delight in the isolation. The Tamar Bridge fastens Cornwall to Devon and England but if a border fence were placed across it, under the cover of darkness in suitably Cornish piratical style, the protests, especially outside the summer season, would be scarce.

The family's first home in Truro was in Falmouth Road, in a large house with its own tennis court, less than a mile from the town centre. Roger attended the primary school nearby, Bosvigo School. He showed an interest in music at a surprisingly early age when he and some school friends formed a skiffle group, The Bubblingover Boys, before his ninth birthday. They performed just once, at a school dance, though none of them could play an instrument in the real sense. Still, organising the practices, soundproofing the family garage with egg-boxes, and strumming a few chords on the ukulele in rough unison with other instruments had warmed Roger to life in a pop group.

In May 1960 he started his first term at Truro Cathedral School. The school was funded by several ecclesiastical charities and had been in existence for more than 400 years. It had only 200 pupils, sixteen of whom were chosen to sing in the choir; Roger Taylor was one of these pupils and had to sing three times on Sundays and at weddings and Midnight Mass at Christmas. Aside from an inclination to Latin and Religion, it was otherwise an ordinary, if select, school, teaching boys from the age of ten to eighteen. Geoff Pester was also a member of the choir and became a close school friend of Roger, sometimes going with him to the beach, and staying in touch as he progressed through pop groups as a teenager. "I remember him being a good singer," says Pester. "He was an ordinary sort of lad. I don't think you'll find he has any enemies in Truro, he wasn't that type of person. I saw his group The Reaction play at a coffee bar in St Agnes, it was called the 'Hey Griddle Griddle', and Roger was the same as I recalled him at school. He was very quiet but extrovert if you could mix these two together. I noticed early on that he let his feelings go into his music."

Geoff Moore was another regular visitor to the Taylor's and was immediately aware of Roger's fondness for pop music. He remembers trips to Ford's record shop in Truro. Early in 1963 Roger bought a copy of Jet Harris and Tony Meehan's 'Diamonds', an instrumental written around bass and drums which topped the charts. Roger was obsessive about the track and it might have prompted a switch from acoustic guitar to drums as his main instrument. He was already quite proficient on the drums after starting out on a basic kit his dad had bought him for Christmas 1961.

Roger was one of the gang which met along Falmouth Road and tripped through the fields nearby. He was like the other boys except for his accent, which was neither Cornish nor East Anglian. "I suppose it was just posh, he always sounded a bit posh, but he wasn't a toff or anything," said Geoff Moore. During one long summer Roger was shot in the back of the leg as the gang scampered through fields pursued by a zealous farmer's son. "It was only a pellet but it left a bit of a mark," said Geoff. "The lad who shot him was nearly crying, asking us not to tell anyone what he'd done." They would amble for hours along the railway lines, dodging the goods trains, or play tennis on the court next to Roger's house.

In September 1960 Roger switched schools when he was offered a scholarship at Truro School which had been established in the town since 1880. Although it was a public school with boarders, Roger attended as a day boy because he lived nearby. Nearly one-third of the 600 boys at the school had received scholarship grants from the local authority. "It wasn't an up-market public school by any means. It wasn't terribly oppressive at all, most of us had a lot of fun there," said Andy Wright, a classmate of Roger's. The school hymn begins: "High on a hill with a city below..." and the panorama of Truro, the river sweeping into the city and the cathedral standing in pale serenity, is remarkable, viewed from the school grounds above Trennick Lane. The school is a prestigious establishment, housed in an imposing building in its own extensive gardens. It was a place of great happiness for Roger Taylor, who has often spoken of his pride in being an old boy, and still attends functions there. Its motto is Esse Quam Videri which means, 'To be rather than to seem' – or, as the current headmaster, Mr G.A.G. Dodd explains: "In other words, don't just look good but have real values underneath".

During 1963 Roger, still on guitar, formed his first group, Cousin Jacks, which was the old colloquial term for Cornish tin miners or for Cornish people in general. After a few rehearsals he turned finally to drums. They played occasionally at a local Liberal club, sometimes under the name of The Falcons. It was hardly a serious project, but during the year the band was intact Roger learned the rudiments of both drumming and life in a group.

He was an average scholar at a school renowned for its academic excellence. He was quite lethargic, doing merely enough work to get by, already dreaming of London and a life devoted to rock 'n' roll. "We saw early on that Roger was very ambitious with his music," said his mother, Winifred. "I suppose we were hoping the drumming would turn out to be a hobby because it seemed such a waste of his intelligence. Very few people made it as proper musicians and I remember one neighbour saying we must be absolutely furious that Roger was spending such a lot of time running about with his group instead of studying."

As a day boy he wasn't subject to the same level of regimen as the other pupils and his blond hair was soon worn past his collar. The school uniform included a blue blazer and cap which had to be worn at all times out of the school building. It was tradition for pupils to touch the peak of their cap if they came across a teacher.

During his school-days Roger was an extremely frail boy; he was one of the last to properly fill out. He was quiet, though his close circle of friends was already aware of his mischievous sense of humour. "One of my lasting memories of Roger is of us coming off the rugby field," said Andy Wright. "He was absolutely white and shivering like billy-o. Sport just wasn't his thing, he seemed so very frail." After school they would sometimes visit a coffee bar in Old Bridge Street in the centre of Truro and here Roger developed the habit which plagued most future drummers - he began tapping out rhythms on the table until the others would scream out in irritation.

In 1964 his parents separated and he moved with his sister Clare and mother to Hurland Road in Truro, another large detached house with a badminton court in its grounds. At this time Roger formed a trio with two school friends, David Dowding and Michael Dudley. They played solely instrumentals, usually Shadows' covers, since none of them had a microphone. "It struck me right away how good Roger was at playing," said Michael Dudley. "He really was astonishingly good. We used to do 'Wipe Out', The Surfaris' song with all that snare drum and Roger could do it without any problem." Roger befriended Vaughan Hankins who lived in nearby Northfield Drive and was another pupil at Truro School with aspirations to be a drummer. "He used to help me quite a lot," says Hankins. "He had a lot of flair on the drums even then. We never played in the same groups because bands never thought of having more than one drummer in those days."

Word of Roger's ability soon spread and a local group, Johnny Quale and The Reaction, targeted him early in 1965. Michael Dudley, who had immediately established himself as Roger's main musical confidant, also defected to join this more experienced group. The pair had much in common but could hardly have looked more dissimilar; Roger was slight and fair, while Michael was dark and six feet four inches tall.

Johnny Quale's real name was John Grose and he was a few years older than Roger and Michael. He was fundamentally an Elvis Presley impersonator, complete with sideburns, quiff, and a strict adherence to rock 'n' roll. His previous local groups included The Blue Stars and The Strangers, with whom he was known as Johnny King. He tagged himself Johnny Quale after the bird of the same name, though the spelling was different. Also, at this time, a whale was washed up on Perranporth beach and locals dubbed it 'Johnny Whale', which Johnny saw as a sign; if they could remember Johnny Whale, they would do the same with Johnny Quale. The other group members were Jimmy Craven on bass, Graham Hankins on lead guitar and, joining a few months later, John 'Acker' Snell on saxophone.

After just a few rehearsals the band's first show was at the fifth annual 'Rock And Rhythm Championship' in March 1965 organised by the Round Table in Truro City Hall. Fifteen groups entered and performed before a fervent audience of an estimated 800 teenagers. Their cries inspired the headline, 'One Long Scream As Beat Groups Battle It Out' in the *West Briton and Royal Cornwall Gazette*. Johnny Quale and The Reaction came fourth, trailing to The Individuals and The Intruders, both from St Austell, and Three And A Bit from Wadebridge. In the unofficial shouting match, Falmouth's Soundcasters were the winners, bringing with them to Truro a squad of girls with particularly strong lungs.

The placing was much better than The Reaction had expected. They had opened the show and were not sure whether their peculiar mixture of P.J. Proby, Gene Pitney, Elvis Presley, Roy Orbison and Beatles' covers would register much support. "I remember hearing the other bands commenting about Roger," said Johnny Quale. "They must have seen him warming up or something because they were all saying what a great drummer he was, but he was damn good." The singer was going through his P.J. Proby phase, sporting a pony tail and lace-up flies with bells attached to the buttons. Johnny soon noticed Roger's unparalleled popularity with girls. "He had such an angelic face," he said. "In many ways he was really baby boyish. The girls sort of took to him straight away. The rest of us were all quite loud in terms of personalities but he was quiet and I think the girls liked that."

In the autumn of 1965 the band recorded a demo disc at a cinema in Wadebridge. By now, perhaps precipitating the split which came soon afterwards, the band were often playing two sets, one as The Reaction with the various musicians taking turns to sing, and the other as Johnny Quale and The Reaction when Johnny would put on his showman routine. They decided to record an EP, each side of which would be given over to the band in its two disparate forms. The studio was mobile, quite primitive, and set up in a room at the cinema. "It cost us £40 to put the songs on tape and have the records made," said Johnny Quale. "I can't remember what songs we did, but I'm sure Roger sang a James Taylor track. When we finished I think the tape was sent away and some time afterwards we received about a dozen demo discs, I haven't got a clue what happened to them." Almost certainly, this formed Roger Taylor's first studio work and his début on record. It has never appeared in any published discography of the Queen band members and few people aside from the musicians involved and their families know of the record's existence.

Johnny Quale's refusal to play little aside from Elvis Presley songs led to his discharge at the end of 1965, and, indeed, Elvis was indirectly part of his downfall. The band had agreed to keep one particular Saturday night clear of bookings because an Elvis film was to be screened at the Plaza in Truro. It was supposed to be a night out for the group, a break from their usual performance duties, but they were offered a gig at short notice and cancelled the outing. Johnny Quale performed with the band but he was furious. "We played at this dance," he said. "I was committed to the group but I felt let down by them. I was sometimes a bit hot tempered in those days. I'm older and wiser now, it seems such a trivial thing to fall out about now."

A stalwart of the local scene, sausage-maker extraordinaire Roger 'Sandy' Brokenshaw, was handed the microphone instead. Roger was again a few years older and had contacts throughout Cornwall. He convinced them he could sing better than Johnny Quale, had a wider repertoire, and would find the group plenty of bookings at the dances he was co-promoting in the county. He, along with another butcher friend, had already given them a sample of his promotional skills when he booked them a few months earlier to appear in Exeter and Torquay. He assured them a top class hotel would be provided, all covered by the local promoter. They found their hotel beds were still warm and unmade from the previous guests, and in the morning they each had to pay for their own rooms!

The band's name was shortened to The Reaction. By day Roger Brokenshaw worked as a butcher's assistant in Truro. "Roger Taylor used to wait for me outside the butcher's in his school uniform," he said. "He was a very quiet guy. He wasn't the best drummer in the world at that time but he was good. The whole band was, and we got on famously." The butcher's became a common rendezvous for the group before they moved on to rehearsals or concerts. "Roger [Brokenshaw] used to make the sausages," said Michael Dudley. "He was a filthy, greasy bugger and there was a right old smell in there. I don't think I've ate sausages to this day."

Standing at under a foot smaller than Michael Dudley, what he lacked in inches Roger Brokenshaw compensated for in personality. In his multi-coloured sheepskin jacket, with his candy floss curly hair and effusive manner, audiences couldn't fail to notice him. He also possessed a robust voice and his renditions of numbers by James Brown and Otis Redding won The Reaction many admirers. John Snell also provided a distinctive edge to the band since few groups had saxophone players. He was noted too for his goatee beard, a personal tribute to Acker Bilk.

On March 7, 1966, The Reaction were voted the winners of the annual Rock And Rhythm Championship and awarded a silver cup. They made the local paper, this time with a photograph, above a typically downbeat story: 'Accountant Marries Sales Girl'. The roar of the Truro crowd, the spirited music blasted through their Vox amplifiers, their all-black attire (apart, of course, from singer Roger), it meant precious little outside Cornwall, but winning the competition made the world of difference to The Reaction. Most importantly, it was recognition that they were the best band in Cornwall, and bookings came easy from here on. The county trailed the rest of the country in other cultural areas, but it had a thriving pop music scene. There wasn't a lot else to do, so every barn, village hall, coffee bar, and nightclub was putting on groups and there was always a guileless audience on hand to support their efforts.

The Reaction began to play concerts at least three nights a week at venues like PJs in Truro, The Blue Lagoon in Newquay, Flamingo's in Redruth, the Princess Pavilion in Falmouth, the Penzance Winter Garden, and village halls at St Agnes, St Just and Mullion. The Sixties had thrown up a number of enterprising Cornish promoters and The Reaction were often booked as support to relatively big names like The Kinks, Tyrannosaurus Rex, Gerry And The Pacemakers, The Inbetweens, who later became Slade, and a group featuring the young Ritchie Blackmore.

An excellent ally to The Reaction, and later to Smile and Queen, was John Adams. John had left his native Whitby early in the Sixties to pursue a life of sea and surf in Cornwall. He was from a family steeped in business, so when the Penzance Winter Garden came up for sale in 1961, he persuaded the folks back home that it was worth a £12,000 investment and that he would run the place. Seven years later, on a trip to London, he saw both The Doors and Jefferson Airplane and decided to alter the booking policy of The Winter Garden which had hitherto been a bastion of more traditional English seaside amusement. Jethro Tull and Ten Years After were early headliners, for fees of £100 and £125 respectively, and thereafter every Thursday night became 'progressive night' at the 800-capacity hall. The venue on Penzance's promenade became known as 'The Wints' ('The Garden', though preferred by John, didn't catch on quite as well), and was sold out every week. It had its own relaxed atmosphere and cushions were distributed for the punters to sit on.

As a promoter working from England's most southerly point, John Adams soon ran into problems, but contingency plans were at hand. Many bands, especially from the north, considered every venue in the south to be about twenty miles from London. "I remember that happening a lot with the Merseybeat groups," says Adams. "They'd ring us up at about 10 pm, half an hour before they were due to go on, and say they'd soon be with us. I'd ask them where they were and they'd say somewhere like Honiton! [a town north of Exeter, about 100 miles away]." Some bands, aware of the distance involved, would be reluctant to even accept bookings in the south west, so John amalgamated with other promoters and formed an association of ballrooms at Torquay, Plymouth, Cardiff, Redruth and Falmouth; it was then a much more attractive proposition. Unknown to the bands, the different promoters would swap information. If a musician had been a nuisance or reckless, the next venue on the 'tour' was warned so preparations could be made, or the concert pulled altogether.

The Reaction appeared many times in Penzance. They had a large following and although John Adams could not remember their music specifically, he recalled the success of the evenings. Along with a trio called The Blue Caps, they were among only a handful of local bands capable of selling out the venue. Smile also appeared regularly and Queen's first appearance in Penzance, a few months before their first single was released, was as support to Caravan,. "It has stuck in my mind a bit that Queen had that attitude of knowing they were going somewhere," he said. "We had that feeling from them that we were lucky to be having them playing the gig."

The Winter Garden became a thriving live music institution. But in 1979 John left to set up a film and video company called 'The Three S's', dedicated to his three interests in life aside from music - surf, sea and skateboarding. Among his final bookings, each of them a fitting testament to his dynamism, were The Sex Pistols, Talking Heads, The Stranglers and The Ramones. The Winter Garden closed in 1992. Various plans have been forwarded and rejected since but all the while, battered by sea spray and rain, a piece of Cornwall's history slowly rusts away.

Roger Taylor and Michael Dudley formed the core of The Reaction and during 1966 and '67 had, like many teenagers in the UK, moved from the sharp snap of soul to the more complex textures of progressive music played by such acts as Jimi Hendrix and Cream; though, perhaps surprisingly, Roger Taylor had little affection for standard rhythm'n'blues. They picked up a new bass player early in 1966, Rick Penrose, who'd spent four years in another strong Cornish band, The Strangers, who played on the same circuit. He initially joined The Reaction for two shows in Torquay over one weekend, at the Town Hall and the Lansdowne. They liked his style and he was soon asked to become a permanent member.

Roger Brokenshaw, meanwhile, was entrenched in upbeat soul and mainstream ballads. The other band members were beginning to grow suspicious of his accounting, since he was promoting the dances at which they often played. "I think we had the impression that Roger was taking us for a bit of a ride," said Michael Dudley. "Him and his mate were wide boys, but nice enough with it." The rest of the group had a feeling that they had 'grown out' of Roger Brokenshaw. "He was great at first, all that shouting and running about but it was all a bit coarse," said Rick Penrose. "As the music got better we wanted to express ourselves in different ways. Roger was a good showman but he didn't mature in the same way the rest of us did." No one in the group was particularly confident in such a situation so they resorted to a rather tactless stratagem to oust Roger Brokenshaw - they simply forgot to collect him in the van.

Roger Taylor took on vocals in his absence; this was a precursor to his permanent role as the group's singer. After being left waiting on several occasions, Roger Brokenshaw presumably got the message, though he was hardly the type to let it upset him greatly. He returned to the cabaret scene, working by day at the famous Redruth Brewery. After work he transformed into Rockin' Roger Dee in social clubs. With no ambition to leave Cornwall, he became a steadfast on the circuit, still sporting a Teddy Boy jacket, an eager smile, and proud to have been one of the first in the country to use backing tapes in his act.

Trios were suddenly in vogue, so The Reaction's new line-up became Roger Taylor on drums and vocals, Michael Dudley on guitar and Richard Penrose on bass. Ben Daniel, the most recent member on guitar, left without enmity; he had been brought in to allow Michael Dudley to move across to the electric organ. The others had never thought Ben overly committed to the group anyway ('Ben enjoyed moaning a bit' - Rick Penrose). Roger's drum kit was pushed forward and he showed no awkwardness in the spotlight, far from it. Sometimes on a whim they would change the name of the group to The Creation for the night, despite there being another British band of the same name releasing records at that time. Paisley shirts and flares were the standard dress, but in typically reactionary spirit, Roger Taylor's usual stage wear was an electric blue suit complete with a tie. Michael Dudley had long been an admirer of Roger's ability but in the stripped down version of The Reaction, he flourished. "He was always quite a long way ahead of the rest of us, and we were quite good players," he said. "He soon had the Hendrix drum patterns off pat and he really became the centre of attention. He could sing well and was by far the most accomplished."

Rick Penrose was also quietly in awe of Roger's talent: "He was an incredible drummer. Roger had a very, very wonderful sound. He made it look so easy which I think is the sign of a really good musician. I remember we did a gig in Taunton and one of Mike's strings broke. Me and Roger just kept playing and you could hardly notice Mike had dropped out. It was a really full sound."

Paul Martin, then in his teens, saw one of The Reaction's first shows with Roger singing and found the experience profound. He attended the Princess Pavilion almost every week for six years and in that time, when he estimates he saw more than 500 different groups, no performer stayed in his memory the same way as Roger Taylor: "He started singing this soul song, I think it was called 'Walk Me Out In The Morning Dew' and everyone stopped dancing. It was quite unusual, they were actually listening to the music, like they were stunned. He really let himself go into the music, really lit up. I just knew that whatever it was you had to have to make it, he had it, no doubt about that, he had it." He kept a watch on Roger after the show and noticed 'a quiet, loner sort of chap' mingling in the bar. The pair never spoke but Paul Martin kept a note of his face and recognised Roger immediately when he was with Queen nearly a decade later.

After one show in Falmouth, Roger met one of his first girlfriends, Eileen Wright. Eileen was one of 'the Flushing girls' along with Jill Carpenter and Penny Eathorne. The three of them would take the boat to Falmouth across Falmouth Bay from their homes in Flushing to dance away the night at the Princess Pavilion. It was a six mile journey by road, but that way they couldn't look up to the stars and dream. They were the archetypal British groupies, giggly and excitably shy, with starry, romantic notions of the boys from out of town, bearing not even remotely carnal undertones. They singled out Roger immediately. In their typically dismissive estimation there was no competition from the other members of The Reaction. Roger had neat blond hair and soft features which carried more than a trace of mischievousness when he smiled. Perhaps more importantly, they thought he resembled David McCallum, one of the stars of the cult American television series, *The Man From U.N.C.L.E.*.

Eileen became a regular addition to The Reaction's travelling crew and was made to feel at home. She and Roger were still too young to drink in pubs so their dating was limited to coffee bars. However, since Roger played with the band most nights there were very few occasions when the pair were alone together. The distance between them, much of it covered only by quiet rural roads, and neither of them old enough to drive, also made for a perplexing courtship. One memorable date was the time The Who came to town. Roger was by now consumed by the brilliance of Keith Moon, and had adopted Moon's crouched style of playing and painted a target on his bass drum. He had none of the outrageousness but otherwise he saw himself as Cornwall's answer to Keith Moon. The Who appeared at Camborne in the summer of 1965, just a few miles down the A3047 from Redruth. "He talked about Keith Moon a hell of a lot, he thought he was the best drummer in the world," said Eileen. "The Reaction later played 'My Generation' at their gigs. At the end of the show Keith Moon threw his drumsticks into the audience. Roger tried, but he never caught them. I remember he walked out of the concert on cloud nine, he'd finally seen his idol."

Their relationship wasn't sexual ("It might have been the Sixties and free love and all that, but it hadn't reached Cornwall, or if it had it hadn't reached me" - Eileen) and Eileen found Roger to be a quiet, shy teenager. He rarely spoke of any great desire to become a pop star, in fact, he more often mentioned that he wanted to become a dentist or airline pilot. "He wasn't a raunchy bloke at all," she said. "He was a very gentle person. I've often thought that he must have pushed himself quite a lot to project the image he now has."

During their ten month romance, Eileen scribbled Roger's name on her school books and relished seeing him, but she still held an affection for a boy she had been seeing before Roger, Chris Libby, who lived in Flushing. The long journey to Truro to see Roger was also becoming tiresome. If she caught the bus it meant a four-mile walk at the end through unlit rural lanes. On one occasion an older man made unwelcome advances to her on the bus and it left her distraught. Unexpectedly, Chris Libby contacted her and said he wanted to return some books; she mistakenly saw this as an attempt by him to resume the relationship. At Christmas 1965 she finished with Roger. "He was very upset," she said. "My mum said he cried, but I don't know about that. He used to phone me at my friend's house." Either way, they both spent Christmas without a partner.

Eileen, now working as a nurse for the Blood Transfusion Service, was one of the many acquaintances of Roger Taylor to pack into his Truro show in 1994. Throughout the concert her friends were forever digging her in the ribs and trying to persuade her that the lyrics were about the heartbreak of losing his first love, his Flushing Girl. Eileen still has a sentimental attachment to Roger. "I didn't like it when he wore his sunglasses on stage," she complains. "He looks much better with them off. It was his eyes that I remember him for."

Michael Dudley does not necessarily recall Roger Taylor in the same chaste manner as Eileen Wright. He remembers a steady number of compliant girls, all of them eager to embrace the spirit of the age. Indeed, the band's unspoken accord was to make great music and procure as many women as possible. In summer Roger Taylor and the others would make use of the nearest field for sensual recreation or, when the days were shorter and colder, space would be found in the van. Roger had the most success, he had already discovered the seductive potential of his youthful features and sad blue eyes and the others were secretly envious of his strike rate.

One of Roger's regular girlfriends was Jill Johnson. A former pupil at Truro's County Grammar School for Girls, she spent a year with Roger and was part of the set which followed The Reaction around and hung-out at Truro's coffee bars. Roger and Jill often teamed up with his neighbour Vaughan Hankins and his wife-to-be, Gill Wilton. Vaughan's father owned a garage so getting a car was never a problem. The four would have nights out together at Tregaye Country Club, Flo's Bar in Devoran or at the Pandora Inn at Restronguet on the road to Falmouth. "It was just a normal boy-girl relationship," said Gill. "They got on very well together and seemed quite fond of each other."

Jill Johnson was afterwards part of an all-girl trio called The Three J's. The other members were sisters Pat and Sue Johnstone. One of Roger's first recording sessions was as a back-up musician to The Three J's. The girls, playing guitars and flutes, had been rehearsing with Roger on drums in premises next to the Barley Sheath pub in the centre of Truro. They met Rod Wheatley, the owner of a Ferrograph tape recorder, and he offered to tape some of their songs. Rod was helped by his friend, Grenville Penhaligon, and they put down two songs on two-track tape. "I remember

Roger turning up with these three gorgeous girls with gorgeous voices," he said. "The session wasn't very long, an hour perhaps. The music was very, very good. They certainly had it all together. Roger had to have it all perfectly right, he was very exact about it. It was obvious he had a lot of talent. I clearly recall thinking he was someone of extraordinary capabilities. He wasn't a bighead in any shape or form. Boys from Truro School were rather full of themselves in those days but he was a clever lad with no falseness about him." Jill Johnson, incidentally, forged her own career in music, fronting the folk quartet, The Famous Jug Band, until they split in the early Seventies. They released two albums on Liberty Records, before Jill became ill with agoraphobia and later moved to Canada where her two elder twin sisters already lived.

By 1967 The Reaction had acquired their own back-up team. Enthusiastic rather than particularly experienced or adept, Neil Battersby and Peter Gill-Carey, both also pupils at Truro School, became the semi-official roadies. Neil was elected to drive the group's battered Thames Trader van, complete with four bald tyres, because he was the first in the gang to reach seventeen. He was also trusted to switch on and off the house lights of the various venues they played to complement the group's musical finale.

By now they were indubitably Cornwall's best band, only The Mechanics from St Austell ran them close. They were also receiving reasonable fees for their concerts and Michael Dudley had enough from his share to buy himself a sports car.

Peter Gill-Carey lived with his family in a large, handsome Edwardian house called Penkerris, just a mile or so from the seafront at St Agnes. His father, Dr Michael Gill-Carey, was the village doctor with another practitioner. The Gill-Careys gave visitors a hearty welcome and before long The Reaction were regular performers at their children's parties. These were usually held in late November to mark the birthdays of Peter and his younger sister Susan. The furniture was removed from the dining room, the carpet literally rolled away, and the concerts began. Roger Taylor, even at this stage, was pedantic about his playing; he often went through to the sitting room and warmed up his snare drum by the fire to put it in tune.

Mrs Dorothy Gill-Carey, an ebullient, endearingly bossy woman, was always keen to lend a hand to her son and his friends. She designed a few posters and booked the group to appear at St Agnes Chapel Hall. It was part of an evening of music and drama run by the Women's Institute. "Many of the elderly ladies weren't used to such loud music and several of them took out their hearing aids," she said. The pathos of the evening had no limits as Mrs Gill-Carey insisted they closed with the National Anthem. "They had never played it before, probably never even thought about it but I was adamant that they'd just have to do their best," she said. "It was certainly one of the weirdest renderings I have ever heard." Poor Roger, his cool under mortal threat, suffered the final embarrassment when the assortment of middle-aged and elderly ladies singled him out for special attention, when they admitted a fondness for the 'little blond drummer'.

The Reaction had several rehearsal bases, but for a long time used a caravan parked in the expansive back garden of Michael Dudley's family, also in St Agnes. The other parents admired Mr and Mrs Dudley's tolerance, but were unaware that Michael's devotion stretched to vandalising one of the family's bookcases by using sticky tape to spell out 'The Reaction' on the glass. The caravan burned down several years later, but the bookcase survived, though the 'N' in Reaction lost its fight with gravity and fell off.

Roger Taylor, though his role in the group was never actually discussed, had evolved into the natural leader. He was barely seventeen years old and looked a few years younger, but he willingly shouldered most of the responsibility for running the group. For some time there had been a liaison with a Bodmin booking agency, BCD Entertainments. The agency had been set up in 1962 by Peter Brown and from its offices in Queen's Crescent, Bodmin, concerts were set up throughout the south west. The only other local agency of note was LMD Entertainments in Torquay run by Lionel Digby. Incidentally, although appearing to be acronyms, neither agency name had any real meaning but each had a suitable ring of eminence. Roger argued successfully that The Reaction could find their own concerts and save themselves ten per cent of the fee; they soon parted company with BCD.

Roger often hit upon whimsical ideas which the others were almost duty bound to accept. He acquired his family's piano, took it out of its wooden frame, painted it, and during shows would leave his drum kit to crash out some wanton chords on it. The Reaction would close with a version of Wilson Pickett's 'Land Of 1,000 Dances', complete with a freestyle section where he would attack the keys. He was clearly becoming aware of the importance of the visual aspect of presenting music. The budget was obviously limited so he had to work within certain limitations. At The Flamingo in Redruth they closed their set by spraying each other with soapy foam. Roger then began coating his cymbals with petrol and towards the end of the show they would be lit to blaze merrily for a few minutes. Unfortunately, a rag soaked in petrol fell to the stage floor at a venue in Par, near St Austell, and there was a panic when it looked like the stage was about to catch fire. For a while Roger used two bass drums; it looked impressive, even more so when he put a light into each one.

Much of Roger Taylor's personality, both musical and in general, was formed during this period. The Reaction were a honed unit, the temperaments matched and, unlike previously, there was a real sense of Roger Taylor's vision coming to the fore. He was the youngest member at seventeen and the smallest in physical terms but there was no doubt he was in control. Rick Penrose and Michael Dudley were not compliant merely for the sake of agreement, they had a genuine respect for Roger's ideas; their trust in his opinion was almost absolute. "It was not an ego trip with Roger," said Rick. "He had a real vision. It was better with the three of us, there was less to argue about. We had the same goals and ideals and there wasn't a lot to discuss. Roger had definite ideas and he voiced them. He was ultra-involved." Roger's on-stage demeanour was an expression of his commitment to the group. "He would give it absolutely everything," said Rick. " He was wet with sweat. I remember he used to split the skin on his bass drum because he was so wrapped up in what he was doing."

Life on the road, Cornish roads included, could be fraught; there was a lot of organisation involved, even for a trio, and along the way they would meet a wide variety of people, some sussed, some fascinating, some dull, some downright stupid. "Roger didn't suffer fools, but he was never ruthless or arrogant with them," said Rick. "He wasn't the type to start shouting. He'd keep his opinion to himself at the time and then voice it to us afterwards. He was intelligent and had a nice way of dealing with people. It would usually mean he got his own way but it wasn't done in an obviously manipulative way." Roger Taylor showed few signs of desperation; there were rarely tantrums of frustration or long speeches in the van of how he would one day play drums at the Albert Hall [which he actually did within three years of leaving The Reaction]. His ambition was discernible, but not necessarily articulated, his friends intuitively saw his future success as inevitable.

The breezy Summer Holiday feel of clambering aboard the van, coasting through Cornwall singing along to The Who and The Beatles on the radio, came to an horrific end in February 1967. Roger had recently passed his driving test and insisted he relieved Neil Battersby of his usual duty. The party - Roger, Neil Battersby, Peter Gill-Carey, Michael Dudley, Richard Penrose, Valerie Burrows (later to be Richard's wife) and Marian Little (Michael's then girlfriend) - was travelling along the A30 to a booking at Dobwalls Village Hall, just a mile or so outside Liskeard. They passed through the village of Indian Queens and ran into fog and driving rain on Goss Moor where the road is picked out through marshland and cotton grass. There was suddenly a great collision and the van somersaulted and landed on its roof. "I remember the van turning over, it seemed to happen in slow motion," said Rick Penrose. "There was a deadly silence and then the sound of metal scraping on the road as we slid along."

They had crashed into a fish van left parked without any lights on, only half on the pavement. Roger was flung through the windscreen but miraculously unhurt. Michael Dudley suffered a broken hand and nose, Marian Little a cut chest, and Valerie Burrows internal stomach injuries. "I was covered in glass," said Rick Penrose. "I looked quite a mess. They had to use tweezers to get the glass out of me. For months this glass kept coming out of my skin. If I rubbed my leg I would cut myself because the glass was still underneath it." By far the worst hurt was Peter Gill-Carey who had been sitting with Valerie on his knee in the passenger's seat where most of the impact had taken place. He was lying unconscious in the road, bleeding profusely, with a large tear in his flesh below the left armpit where a door handle had pierced him.

They were taken to the Royal Cornwall Hospital in Truro where it was found Peter's lung had been punctured and collapsed. Over the course of the night he was given nine pints of blood. Peter's father, Dr Michael Gill-Carey, travelled to the hospital but Dorothy Gill-Carey had to stay at Penkellis to look after their other children. She was told that the chances of Peter surviving were slim. She spent the night shivering next to a raging fire in the grand sitting room, the same room which had rung with the laughter and joy of Peter and his musical friends just a few weeks earlier.

Peter Gill-Carey made a slow, protracted recovery. He was transferred to Frenchay Hospital in Bristol where he underwent several skin grafts to properly close the wound. He missed the whole of 1967 and was not discharged from hospital until the beginning of 1968. He had to study for his 'A' Levels from his hospital bed. Although the impact had been on his left side, he was left with an immobile right hand. Before the accident he had been provisionally accepted to study medicine at Guy's Hospital, London. He learned to write with his left hand and a later operation enabled him to use the thumb of his right hand but he was deemed unfit to become a doctor. Medicine had always been his coveted vocation but he switched to accountancy.

Although Roger Taylor had no physical injury, he suffered psychologically for some time afterwards. Everyone, including Dorothy Gill-Carey, absolved him of any guilt but he was obviously distraught, though he mainly kept it to himself. "We were younger then and able to bounce back from that sort of thing," said Rick. "We just decided to get on with it, it was no one's fault." Roger's father, Michael Taylor, reportedly spent the night of the accident walking the cliffs, something he did often when the family was beset by troubles.

As he had driven the group's van into the back of another vehicle, Roger was technically at fault and charged by police, with an order to appear at Bodmin Magistrates' Court when the papers had been prepared. The question of whether the fish van owner, a Mr Gerald Broad of Shutta Road, East Looe, had been negligent in abandoning his vehicle unattended and without lights on such a dark, wet night was chiefly a civil matter, later to be battled out as an insurance settlement which took seven years to resolve. "All this was ghastly for Roger," said Mrs Gill-Carey. "We, of course, wanted to blame the owner of the fish van but naturally he wanted to blame the group with their old van loaded with equipment and being driven by a seventeen year old. Poor Roger had a cloud over his head - would he be blamed for the accident? I didn't understand the workings of the law but seven years? I could perhaps accept seven months, even seventeen months, but how do they justify seven years? At the end the van owner was eventually blamed and the years of torment were over for Roger." The police still decided to prosecute Roger and during the autumn of 1968 he was found guilty of a driving offence. He did not attend the hearing because he was studying in London.

The road accident came at the worst possible time for the group. They were each studying for their 'A' levels – Michael Dudley wanted to read chemistry at Oxford University and Roger had decided finally to work towards becoming a dentist. The distress might have affected Roger's studies since his 'A' level grades in Biology, Chemistry and Physics were not as high as expected – a disappointment to his father who again walked the cliffs. Michael Taylor, by now working as a driving test examiner, had a reputation for eccentricity. He once broke his leg when he fell from a motor-cycle he was riding around the back garden! Roger's 'A' Level grades, however, were still impressive enough to earn him a place at the London Hospital Medical School.

Futuristic Manifesto

Chapter III

Queen

Hampton is a small town in Middlesex, south-west of London, one of scores clinging roughly to the Thames as it snakes its way past the streets and national landmarks and, eventually, fields, out to the North Sea. Brian May was born in Hampton, at Gloucester House Nursing Home, on July 19, 1947, to Harold and Ruth May. The family home was a few miles away in Feltham, a town of similar size, but composed mainly of families a few notches down the social scale, though the May home was a typical, suburban semi-detached in a quiet cul-de-sac.

There is a continual grumble and roar in the sky above Feltham because it lies close to Heathrow Airport. Its economy has developed in unison with the airport; it has, for example, three times as many council houses as nearby Whitton. The baggage handlers, cleaners, taxi drivers and restaurant staff usually settle in Feltham and walk the streets oblivious to the 747s by their rooftops.

As an only child Brian May was extremely close to his parents. His father was a draughtsman with the Ministry of Aviation and they shared many similar interests. One of Brian May's earliest loves was science fiction comics, the art and graphics of which, along with their peculiar prose, was to later influence his music.

His early musical development began with the ukulele, an instrument his father could play reasonably well. He immediately showed an aptitude and on his seventh birthday he was given an acoustic guitar. Brian May was of the same technical mind as his father, and they both set about altering the guitar to suit his needs. The 'action' [the distance from the strings to the fret board] was narrowed to make it easier to play, and by using copper wires and magnets they made the guitar electric and Brian amplified it by using a home-made wireless. The pair also made a telescope together so Brian could watch the stars above London and Devon, where they went on family holidays. Another of their shared hobbies was photography and before the age of ten Brian was developing his own pictures.

Their tidy house in Walsham Road had an upright piano in the living room and Brian often played it. He was encouraged to do so and took piano lessons, eventually reaching grade four. He was extraordinarily adept on the guitar and applied a relentlessly logical approach to the instrument, listening to songs by performers such as Lonnie Donegan and Buddy Holly and transplanting the chords on to his guitar. The Crickets, at this point, were his favourite group. He was bewitched by their harmonies and the atmosphere of their records. He was soon picking out the notes married to the chords and forming a definite lead style.

Brian was an exemplary scholar and in 1958 left Cardinal Road Infants' School to take up a scholarship at Hampton Grammar School. The all-boys school had nearly 1,000 pupils and was recognised as the best of three local grammar schools, the others being Chiswick Grammar and Latimer Grammar. Hampton Grammar, now known simply as Hampton School, was based in Hanworth Road on roughly the same site as the local mixed comprehensive school, The Rectory, and an exclusive all-girls school, The Lady Eleanor Holles School. When he became a pupil at Hampton it had a reputation for austerity. The head teacher, George Whitfield, believed in a pugnaciously formal approach, full uniform, including caps, had to be worn at all times. Even today the school maintains many of its rigid values. A polite inquiry as to any prevailing memories of Brian May draws forth the formal, two line response: 'Our policy is not to discuss old boys of the School except with those introduced to us by the old boys concerned. I would therefore suggest that you approach Brian May directly,' – G G Able, MA (Cantab) MA (Dunelm), Headmaster [underlined]. "There was a great emphasis on getting to university, preferably a redbrick one, and sod a career," said a former pupil. "Careers seemed to be an afterthought, there was such an emphasis on academic achievement. Thinking back though, it was a brilliant education. It was fairly strict for sure but the standards were extremely high."

It was apparent immediately that Brian was an exceptional pupil. He could hardly have been otherwise, such was the support from his parents. They had an unusual level of devotion to their son and were simultaneously assenting and solicitous. His friends remember the May household as quiet, sober and a friendly place to be; Harold May was always keen to join in with his son's projects and Ruth May was on hand to supply the tea and biscuits. Brian's love of astronomy was such that he was already planning a career involving the subject, and he excelled at related studies like maths and physics. At Hampton he was placed in the top stream in his year and had to take compulsory Latin.

In the late Fifties the acoustic guitar was an essential fashion item for many teenage boys. For most it was slung conspicuously across the shoulder, a useful prop for a chat with the girls they fancied down at the coffee bar. Even the starched atmosphere at Hampton Grammar School could not repress this teenage musical exuberance. In fact, two pupils Jim McCarty and Paul Samwell-Smith, later became members of The Yardbirds while they were still at the school. Brian May began meeting with others at lunch times where they would strum their guitars. He was the most advanced, and impressed his peers one afternoon with a remarkably faithful rendition of Guy Mitchell's 'Singing The Blues'.

It was fated that Brian would fuse his interest in music and technology and along with a school friend, Dave Dilloway, he began to record songs. Using two tape recorders they would constantly record from one to the other, layering extra parts down on to tape. They used guitars and a bass guitar Dave had made himself, and for percussion tapped out rhythms using bits of Meccano. Harold May became their recording assistant, soldering together pieces of wire, keeping a check on the levels, and allowing them to use the family record player as a surrogate amplifier. They mainly recorded instrumentals, covers of numbers by The Shadows or The Ventures.

High quality American-made Fender and Gibson guitars were filtering through to Britain's music shops by the early Sixties. They were highly desirable, if expensive, and really marked out the difference between spirited amateurs and those aspiring to professionalism. The May family, with some sacrifice, could have afforded to buy Brian such an exquisite guitar, but the imagination of both Brian and Harold May had been fired by the arrival of this sleek wood and mechanical technology. They decided to build their own guitar and their efforts during the autumn of 1963 were to form one of rock's most repeated and enduring anecdotes.

Their earnest endeavour could have been lifted from one of the diagram-by-diagram explanations in *Look And Learn*, the classic children's magazine of the Fifties and Sixties dedicated to the wonderment of science and nature. In short, the neck was carved from a mahogany fireplace; the tension of the strings was balanced by motorcycle valve springs; the tremolo arm was a discarded knitting needle and the fretboard markers were mother-of-pearl buttons borrowed from Ruth May's sewing box. Their only real compromise was to buy a set of three Burns pick-ups, though they were modified by the application of epoxy resin. The finished guitar, which cost £17 10s, was christened 'The Red Special' by Brian because of its deep red colour when polished. Later it also became known as 'The Fireplace'. Their meticulously scientific approach meant that the guitar had a unique tonality which even the most expensive guitars could not emulate. The final testimony to the brilliance of their labours was that the guitar was built to last; it formed much of Queen's sound down the years and has never been discarded. "They kept showing me the Red Special as they worked through it," said Dave Dilloway. "It was a brilliant piece of workmanship. They had no guidelines, they had to do it as they went along. It was not the easiest guitar to play, it has a very thick neck, but it has seen Brian through his career. I tried to make one but it was a plank compared to Brian's."

Dave Dilloway was extremely close to Brian. They were in the same class at school and spent much of the weekend at each other's houses. Dave would travel over to Feltham from his home in Whitton, near Twickenham. Every weekend they would spend at least four or five hours 'making noises' with their instruments. "I remember Brian loved The Temperance Seven," he said. "They were an American style group that played what you'd call trad jazz. It was very Vaudeville. He used to buy their LPs as soon as they came out. Brian had very broad tastes. There was a large collection of classical LPs at his house which belonged to his parents. On the same day I recall him once buying LPs by Julian Bream and Jimi Hendrix and playing bits from both of them on his guitar."

The lunch time guitar club at Hampton became the meeting place for pupils interested in forming groups. Up to ten potential guitarists would converge on an empty classroom and show one another new chord progressions they had learned. By far the best players were Brian May, known to the others as 'Brimi', and Pete Hammerton, known universally as 'Woolly', though no one could remember why. "Brian was pretty shy but he didn't mind playing in front of people," said Dave Dilloway. "He didn't make a big deal about it, he certainly wasn't a show-off. To me, even when Queen made it later on, Brian had to work hard at being on stage. He always seemed just a fraction away from being embarrassed by it all."

Dave Dilloway and Brian May decided to form a group and their first real collaboration with others involved two classmates, Bill Richards on vocals and guitar and John Sanger on piano. Sanger nonchalantly offered his services in class, though it was some time before they realised his piano playing was actually quite advanced. During their earliest shows he played a mini harmonium which was difficult to amplify and the only sound the others could hear emanating from it was the constant roar of the motor. "I had learned to play piano scales and some classical and was thoroughly fed up with it, so I was glad to join a group," said John Sanger. "Everyone seemed to be in and out of bands at the time. Various people were coming together and it was just a fun thing."

Bill Richards had been taught to play guitar by Brian May who had been a major force in his introduction to music. "We were interested in blues and pop and sought inspiration from Brian who was seen as an expert both in terms of his musical knowledge and his playing skill," said Bill Richards. "I was keen to provide vocals for Brian and Dave, for anything from Benny Hill to The Beatles, from The Mojos to Manfred Mann." One of the earliest songs in their repertoire was The Moody Blues' hit, 'Go Now' which they were able to emulate well by virtue of having a pianist.

As an early example of Brian May's pursuit of excellence, he asked Bill Richards to buy himself a better guitar. "There was a problem with my guitar which was cheap and nasty," said Bill, "It fell to Brian to tell me tactfully that if I couldn't get another one I would have to leave. I couldn't, so I left. To be honest, I think Brian was being even more tactful by underplaying the problem with my vocals, which weren't right at the time, although he was kind enough to say much later that I'd sorted it out." Another Hampton schoolmate, Malcolm Childs, replaced Bill Richards but he lasted barely a week ("He liked the idea of being in a group but was unreliable about almost everything," - Dave Dilloway). Finally, they settled on John Garnham, a rhythm guitar player who had played several concerts with other local groups. He had his own equipment and was already a fine player.

They advertised for a drummer by putting up a postcard in the window of Albert's, Twickenham's only music shop. Richard Thompson, from nearby Hounslow, called at Dave Dilloway's house and after a quick chat he became the group's drummer. Richard, a former pupil at Spring Grove Grammar School in Isleworth, had played drums for three years, most recently with The Fifth Column who had appeared several times at youth clubs in the Hounslow area.

They found their singer at a dance at Murray Park Hall in Whitton. While they were watching the main group, Chris And The Whirlwinds, they recognised another Hampton pupil, Tim Staffell. Tim was watching the band and, true to blues mythology, playing along with a mouth organ. Both Dave and Brian were standing close to Tim and could discern that his playing was in tune and fairly proficient. They knew his face from school, and later found out he was in the year below them. He had already been playing with another local band, The Railroaders, but decided to join Dave and Brian's group. "The infrastructure seemed better," said Tim. "In Dave Dilloway I think they had a central sense of organisation, he was always knocking together speakers and setting up rehearsals. I think they were compatible with my character. They both had pretty laid back personalities and were respectful of other people."

Tim Staffell's introduction to pop music had been chiefly through Radio Luxembourg, which, along with Radio Caroline, was the first real manifestation of a media specifically for teenagers. He had built his own crystal set and spent hours listening to scratchy songs by the likes of Bobby Vee. In 1961 he had been involved in a serious road accident and spent many weeks off school while his broken legs healed. He missed much of his education and returned demoralised, unable to catch up with the rest of his class. He adopted a fairly lax approach to school afterwards, already quite sure his vocation would be artistic rather than academic. His outlook made him the antithesis of Brian May and Dave Dilloway. "I was more irresponsible in the sense that I was more responsive to trivia, street culture, that sort of thing," he said. "I'd lived a less sheltered life than them. There was an element of Bohemia I suppose." Dave Dilloway also recognised that he was fundamentally different. "Tim was more off beat, more artistic," he said. "Afterwards he went to art college while we went to university. He was more fashionable. He was keen, quite perky and full of ideas. He was quite a driving force, more than we were."

After much thought, they named themselves 1984. George Orwell's bleak, ashen prose of newspeak, doublethink, Thought Police and Big Brother had been a major influence on a generation. '1984' was the band's shorthand for a time of institutionalised melancholy; it was an ideal name for a pop group. "We liked it because it was futuristic, simple, something catchy and different," said Dave Dilloway. "Me and Brian had thought of hundreds of names, it was a hobby in itself in a way. When we weren't doing that we were doodling on our school books, drawing guitars all the time." Other contenders as names included the far inferior Bod Chappie And The Beetles and The Mind Boggles.

During these raw, formative days, there was already evidence of ideas which would be developed many years later. In choosing the name 1984, both Dave Dilloway and Brian May were mindful that the group could be thematic, existing on several levels. "We toyed with the idea of writing a mini-rock opera about 1984," said Dave. "We talked about what stage sets we'd have and the lighting we'd use. As kids we would not have been able to generate the finance but if someone had come along and invested in us I think we could have been up there, we could have been something like Pink Floyd. We were a good team. I was quite technical, Tim was artistic and Brian was the musical brain." The 'rock opera' was never more than a fanciful proposal, at this stage they hadn't written a single original song, but it was testimony to lively imaginations.

1984 were fortunate to be located within the boundaries of Richmond Borough Council since it had a progressive view on youth and music. The early Sixties had been notorious for street violence as the message of rebellion from US rockers like Jerry Lee Lewis and Elvis Presley was wilfully misunderstood. On the silver screen it was slick Americanised choreography but the ersatz British version was a scowling Teddy Boy and a territorial viciousness. Councillors in Richmond avoided the usual platitudes, and instead formed the Whitton Beat Club. In one swoop, they effectively disarmed the threat of rock'n'roll and institutionalised it in a delightful, suburban British manner. Mr Connisbee, a middle-aged man with experience as a Cub Scout leader, administered Whitton Beat Club. Groups were charged 10s per annum and thereafter were allowed to use youth clubs and schools in the Richmond area to rehearse. 1984 were allocated Chase Bridge Primary School in Twickenham, just a drop goal away from the nearby rugby ground. Brian May would usually be taken to rehearsals by his dad in the Jowett Javelin car he owned.

Chris Whittome-Knights, a friend of a friend, was the first to consider 1984 ready for their début concert. He booked them to appear in a hall across the road from St Mary's Church in Twickenham on October 28, 1964, and promised them a very reasonable fee of £10. John Garnham was the only member of 1984 with a driving licence and vehicle so his tiny bubble car became weighed down with instruments and amplifiers as he ferried their equipment to the venue. The concert was a qualified success and another followed soon afterwards at Richmond Grammar School for Girls; three members of 1984 had girlfriends at the school and they had prompted the booking.

The members of 1984 were avid music fans and though they were only in their mid-teens they perused the different venues in west London, anxious to learn from bands on the circuit. A big influence on them was a group formed by older boys from Hampton School called The Others, led by Pete Hammerton, who had recorded a brilliantly raucous single for Fontana Records, 'Oh Yeah' in 1964. There was frequent interchange of personnel between The Others and 1984, and when Brian May and Pete Hammerton shared the same stage it was regarded as a treat on the local scene. Many felt The Others shaded 1984; their sharp, raw R&B, built on The Rolling Stones' maracas shuffle, was certainly highly authentic. Brian May and Tim Staffell were regulars at Eel Pie Island, a concert hall off the bank of the Thames in Twickenham, and they also travelled out to the Station Hotel in Richmond. The scene was burgeoning with talent and in the space of a few months they saw nascent musical legends like The Yardbirds and The Rolling Stones at extremely close quarters.

Their own concert diary began to fill up steadily and 1984 soon found themselves playing at least one gig each week. They recognised that Brian was their most talented member, and in fact speculated several times that he might be 'poached', but the seat of power within the band was ambiguous. "I probably did as much of the organising as anyone, but it was a committee rather than anything autocratic," said Dave Dilloway. "There was no real strong focal point. We'd all sort out bookings, it would really depend on which one of us was asked. Nothing was ever written down and it was done pretty much word of mouth."

Richard Thompson felt the group's strength lay in the vocal harmonies. "We were just a normal cover versions band but the singing impressed me most," he said. "Tim had a strong voice and was also a very good harmonica player.

The harmonies from Brian and John were excellent. They were a friendly bunch. I suppose I was the outsider because I didn't go to the same school, but it didn't feel that way. We played pretty straight music. We used to listen to Pink Floyd, and Cream were influential later on but at the beginning we were into Chuck Berry and people like that."

The teen groups of the mid-Sixties were the early pioneers of rock music in a group format. There was very little subtlety or guile and most were run on effervescence and spontaneity. Inevitably, as in any novel genre, there was confusion about the ground rules. Many bands became almost Vaudevillian in their approach, believing they should put on a good, lively show at all costs; introspection in its many forms was to arrive several years later. 1984 soon developed a theatrical bent. "We did jokey things, it was all very schoolboyish," said Tim Staffell. "We'd have daft little props like shaving foam and polystyrene bricks. It was an expression of naïveté. I think we thought people would be impressed with that sort of thing and remember us as a good act. We were competing with lots of other teenage bands to make a bit of dough on Saturday night. It was all very lightweight and frothy."

One of their regular bookings was at the Thames Boat Club on the river at Putney. Sometimes they played for up to three hours and their equipment was excellent for a local band; Brian May bought his amplifier from the wages of two summer jobs, one working in a factory making windscreen wipers and the other, as a clerk at a fire extinguisher company.

Brian May did not neglect his studies and when he left Hampton Grammar School in the summer of 1965 he had ten 'O' Levels and four 'A' Levels in physics, maths, applied maths and additional maths. He had been an exemplary pupil, committing himself to a wide range of school activities. He was a member of the dramatics society and his first stage role was as a woman, Lydia Languish in Sheridan's *The Rivals*. This was followed by another role as a woman – a proverbial necessity at an all-boys' school – Lady Mary Lazenby in *The Admirable Crichton*. Brian May was also a member of the school choir, secretary of the debating society, and a senior prefect. His academic brilliance led to him being offered an open scholarship in physics at London's Imperial College of Science and Technology.

Brian's achievement made a four paragraph story in the *Middlesex Chronicle* where it was revealed the scholarship would amount to £75 per year.

It was apparent that the nature of 1984 would alter significantly as they went into higher education. They were all from respectable middle-class homes and there was no question that they would eschew their education for the group. Still, they were too devoted to actually split up, so resolved to adopt a different approach. John Sanger, though he was to rejoin several years later, left ostensibly on a permanent basis when he took up a degree course in technology at Manchester University. He had played just a handful of concerts before his departure. "I had no grand plans to become a star musician, music was a sideline," he said. "At that stage, I would have thought, of them all, that Brian had the makings of being a success in music."

Tim Staffell was accepted on a graphics course at Ealing College of Art, so it meant he and Brian May were still in close proximity and could continue with 1984. Dave Dilloway was reading electronics at Southampton University but travelled to west London most weekends on his motorcycle to arrange songs with them. They also sent cassettes to each other with new parts for songs and vocal harmonies they wanted to rehearse when they reunited. Brian May started at Imperial College in October 1965, studying physics and infra-red astronomy. A large part of his college work was dedicated to interferometry, the study of dust in the solar system.

Although their gigging was now curtailed, 1984 were still intermittently back on the roads around west London at the beginning of 1966, playing covers of Rolling Stones, Beatles, Yardbirds and Spencer Davis songs. On their version of 'Yesterday' Brian would sing the lead vocals and the other band members, already impressed by his guitar playing, were astounded by his strong singing voice. Sometimes they were duty bound to play marathon shows, providing the entertainment at functions from 7 pm to 1 am, during which time they would perform up to 50 songs, and drummer Richard Thompson was asked to play lengthy solos to fill in time. On one occasion they supported a snake dancer and had to share dressing room space with the reptile. Brian used his contacts at Imperial College and 1984 often played there, usually in a different hall but on the same night as relatively established groups like Marmalade, Steampacket and Tomorrow.

Dave Dilloway was able to commit himself more fully to 1984 when he left his university course after just one year. He had not taken to the heavily theoretical nature of the course and opted instead to study for an HND in electronics at Twickenham College of Technology. He had found work with Electronic Instruments Ltd in Richmond and it agreed to sponsor his studies.

While he was on the course he met some students who were attached to Thames Television. They were looking for a group to help them practise their sound engineering. Dave volunteered the services of 1984 and during the spring of 1967 they spent a day at the television studios in Broom Road, Teddington. They recorded a dozen songs, ten of them covers, the other two different versions of a Brian May/Tim Staffell composition called 'Step On Me'. "It was a very large studio, big enough for an orchestra," said Dave Dilloway. "We did all the songs in the space of an evening. Brian liked to get his bits right and he stopped a few times to re-tune his guitar. It was good fun, there was no pressure on us."

The tape was an excellent snapshot of 1984, except the main sound engineer placed far too much emphasis in the mix on John Garnham's rhythm guitar, to the point of obscuring many of Brian May's lead runs. At one point on the tape, John Garnham can be heard advising the engineer to turn up his guitar because he is about to play some lead. In the background, Brian May can be heard shouting, 'Oh, you bastard' as he realises he is to be buried even deeper in the mix.

Brian May was back in a recording studio in April 1967 when he was invited to play on some songs recorded by his old school friend, Bill Richards. Bill had formed the folk/rock group, The Left-Handed Marriage in 1965 with Jenny Rusbridge, Henry Deval and Terry Goulds. Unlike Brian, who was absorbed by the notion of the group format, Bill Richards wanted to establish himself primarily as a songwriter. He had spent his childhood surrounded by classical music and with The Left-Handed Marriage as his vehicle, he wanted to write songs merging the techniques of classical scores with the undiluted pop of The Beatles. In the event, the group concocted modest, whimsical pop in the mode of Al Stewart or Donovan.

In January 1967 the group released the album, 'On The Right Side Of The Left-Handed Marriage'. Only 50 copies were pressed on vinyl since its main function was to attract interest from music publishers. Soon after its release a British publisher (whom Bill Richards steadfastly refuses to name, though Dave Dilloway remembers as Ardmore & Beechwood) did indeed contact him. Brian Henderson, an auxiliary member of the British psychedelic group, Nirvana, had connections with the company and he championed Bill Richards' talents. He suggested that some of the tracks should be re-recorded and Richards, realising the music needed 'thickening', sent a letter to Brian May's home in Belmont Grove, Chiswick, inviting him to guest in the studio. "He wrote to me to say he'd liked the tape I'd sent him and hoped we would be favoured with connubial bliss!" said Bill Richards.

Originally Brian May planned to invite the rest of 1984 to perform on the session at a small studio in Twickenham scheduled for April 4, 1967, but, in the event, only he played. He provided guitar and backing vocals to four songs: 'I Need Time', which later became 'Give Me Time' when it was discovered a song of the same name had already been recorded by someone else; 'She Was Once My Friend'; 'Sugar Lump Girl'; and 'Yours Sincerely', the latter being fundamentally a backwards re-run of 'Give Me Time' with lyrics borrowed from the Russian writer, Pushkin.

The strength of the tracks encouraged the publishers to invest some money in The Left-Handed Marriage and they were booked into the prestigious Abbey Road Studios in London's St John's Wood on June 28. Again, Brian May was asked to contribute and this time he was joined by Dave Dilloway. They were driven to the session by Terry Gould's dad in a Commer van and were met at the studio by an A&R man from the publishing company who failed to spot Brian May's competence. In fact, he was completely nonplussed. "He certainly didn't know a good guitarist when he saw one," said Bill Richards. "He was sardonic and showed no appreciation of Brian's skills. Someone mentioned a solo Brian had played and this A&R man said, 'Solo? What solo?' We didn't know whether he meant it was too short to be called a solo or whether he was being sarcastic." They recorded just two tracks, 'I Need Time' and 'She

Was Once My Friend'. "The publishers stayed interested," said Bill Richards. "They said, 'Don't worry, boy, we think you've got a good group. Just leave it to us. Somebody's got to be interested. If EMI don't want it, we'll take it somewhere else."

Brian May's work with The Left-Handed Marriage became more protracted than first expected but he had pointed out in his first letter to Bill Richards that he would help them 'on the understanding that it wouldn't interfere with his commitment to 1984'. Once more the publishers called for another visit to the studio, so on July 31, 1967, The Left-Handed Marriage, now augmented by bassist/pianist John Frankel and drummer Peter Trout as well as Brian May, recorded at London's Regent Sound Studios. They laid down three songs, 'I Need Time', 'She Was Once My Friend' and a song Bill Richards had written on a trip to Devon, 'Appointment'. None of Bill Richards' songs were ever placed with an artist and he and Brian May drifted apart after they had met for the last time at Bill's wedding in February 1969. Bill is now the head teacher at a secondary school in Buckinghamshire.

Among his group of close friends, Brian May developed a reputation for forgetfulness and meticulousness. "He was a fiddler, it took him an awful long time to get his amplifier right, and his tuning," said Dave Dilloway. "He was forever trying to get his sound dead right. He played a lot of the gigs facing the wrong way. He'd have his back to the audience as he twiddled the knobs on his amplifier. Like a lot of very clever people he was not always one hundred per cent worldly. He was fairly forgetful, his mind was on higher things if you like. He was not a mad professor type, but he could never remember where he'd left his coat."

In fashion terms, Brian May trailed the rest of 1984, who were all moderately cool in their polka dot shirts and jackets heavy with brass buttons. Richard Thompson and Tim Staffell would regularly embark on shopping trips to Carnaby Street and the King's Road. In September 1967 the band entered a talent competition at Croydon's Top Rank club and Brian wore a Royal Marine jacket he had picked up at Chelsea market. It was the boldest fashion statement he had ever made and the others expressed mild surprise. "Brian was always open-minded with ideas but he was straight in the sense of being fairly conventional," said Dave Dilloway. "He was probably late in becoming aware of fashion, he was straight all through the hierarchy of school. I think he managed to sit on the fence for quite some time and had a constant dilemma between his straight and unconventional side. He was into all the music and everything but he was also serious about his studies."

The haircuts in 1984 were basically Beatles mop tops, grown out slightly, so they were acceptable to both their parents and peers. Brian kept his the neatest. It was to be a few years before he discovered perming lotion and adopted a bubbly haircut, perhaps to soften his rather angular and spindly physique. The Beatles haircut was then gone for ever, replaced by a shaggy look which, like his famous guitar and arched playing posture, was to become an authentic rock outline.

At their heat of the talent competition, 1984 played just four songs, The Everly Brothers' 'So Sad (To Watch Good Love Go Bad)', Jimi Hendrix's 'Stone Free', Buddy Knox's 'She's Gone' and Eddie Floyd's 'Knock On Wood'. They were voted the winners and won a reel of Scotch tape and a CBS album each. Tim Staffell claimed Simon and Garfunkel's 'Sound Of Silence', while Brian had to make do with a Barbra Streisand LP. The *Middlesex Chronicle* ran a piece about their success and Brian provided a typically solemn comment: "We want to be able to play well enough to respect ourselves." Unfortunately 1984 were not the overall national victors in the contest so missed out on the first prize of a recording contract with CBS Records, the competition sponsors.

Their home-spun dreams of winning the talent competition paled in May 1967 when they were asked to support Jimi Hendrix at Imperial College. 'Hey Joe' and 'Purple Haze' had already been Top Ten hits and the concert came just two days after the release of his third consecutive smash, 'The Wind Cries Mary'. Brian Jones of The Rolling Stones was backstage with Hendrix, looking particularly gaunt and sickly, but it was nevertheless an early tinge of glamour for 1984. There was actually a fleeting contact with Jimi Hendrix when he opened his dressing room door as they passed and asked Tim Staffell: "Which way's the stage, man?"

Some music business types (no one bothered to ask their names or actual job titles) saw 1984 appear at the London School of Economics in the autumn of 1967 and were impressed. "We were a cut above your average local band and by then we were quite slick I suppose," proffers Dave Dilloway. These 'pleasant enough characters' told 1984 they were involved in the promotion of a massive concert, 'Christmas On Earth', to be held at the Olympia in Kensington just two days before Christmas. Although the concert was to feature a bevy of famous names, among them Jimi Hendrix, Pink Floyd, Tyrannosaurus Rex and Traffic, they were convinced they could find a half hour spot for 1984.

The day of the concert began felicitously when the band were given a clothing budget and taken to Carnaby Street to buy stage gear. They signed a contract of sorts, promising, they believed, that they would remain with their new benefactors if their performance that night brought forth a record deal. Their planned set would focus mainly on soul covers and, as a mark of respect to a fellow performer also on the bill, they decided to drop the Jimi Hendrix covers.

December 23, 1967, turned out to be a lifetime in a day for 1984, a day when they were unequivocally inducted into the mean realities of life as a novice rock group. They arrived at the venue at 3 pm as arranged. During the afternoon and early part of the evening they had to wait patiently, ever so patiently, while bands higher on the bill fastidiously ran through their sound checks. Another snare drum crack, another swamp of echo, another 'one, two, one two' on the mike. It seemed interminable. They were led to the stage at 1 am, only to learn it was a false call. Eventually, fourteen hours after their first arrival, they took the stage at 5 am without a sound check – as the fifteenth band on the bill – and played to an audience already feeling the first pangs of a hangover from their excesses of a few hours earlier.

They were 'pretty knackered' but gave what they considered a reasonable performance. When they left the stage they discovered their money had been stolen from the dressing rooms and their vans and cars had been towed away by police. "We were all tarted up, in make-up, with our hair done and we had to walk the three or four miles to the police compound in Hammersmith," said Dave Dilloway. "Our coats were in the cars, so we were freezing as well. I remember we had to do our Christmas shopping the next day, practically falling asleep. I look back on it now as an adventure." After the concert, incidentally, 1984 saw no more of their recently discovered patrons but were content to get 'some decent clothes out of it.'

Brian May's interest in 1984 was beginning to wane. He relished his university course, he was drawing close to his finals, and although an excellent degree was almost assured, he was still keen to absorb himself in studies. He was heavily involved in a project to observe zodiacal light in Switzerland and supervised the building of a hut on a mountain called Testa Grigia, near the Matterhorn. He also built his own spectrometer and spent time in the hut making observations until the extremely cold weather made it impossible to work.

There were no scenes with the members of 1984 when Brian May announced he was leaving. He promised to remain with them or stand-in temporarily until they found a replacement. "We were only doing it for the fun and a bit of pocket money," said Dave Dilloway. "Even if someone had offered us a record contract I'm not sure we would have taken it. I would have been very tempted to stay in my day job. At that time I wasn't really one for taking risks. Even at the end we were just a covers band, we were happy with that, although Brian and Tim might have wanted to do more of their own stuff. It wasn't a big deal though. Brian would put some ideas forward and if we didn't like them he'd change them slightly or just leave it."

Richard Thompson recalls Brian May and Tim Staffell introducing their own songs at rehearsals. "I think they wrote about three or four numbers," he said. "It was an issue that was never pushed. Their songs were excellent, full of little harmonies. I didn't think they'd come up with a number 1 hit, but it certainly wasn't any old rubbish. There was some good ideas in there but they were nothing like Queen songs."

Watching Brian May's rapid musical development, the others covertly believed he had grown out of 1984. "1984 was never a real search for stardom for any of us," said Dave Dilloway. "We weren't out to break the world of pop, where Smile had those intentions, and Queen definitely did."

Tim Staffell, who had quickly learned to play lead guitar with no small degree of skill, took over from Brian May and also continued to sing. Tim fronted 1984 for about eight months before he also left, to form a new group with Brian. He had considered 1984 without Brian May as a 'rather dull band'. "1984 always existed in an environment of change because we were all on the cusp of leaving school and going to college," said Tim Staffell. "It meant we all knew we would have to readjust, so ultimately 1984 was on a hiding to nothing."

Brian May and Tim Staffell kept in close contact and it would appear that Brian was the catalyst for their collaborative song writing. "Brian was the first to write a song on his own," said Tim Staffell. "He presented it to 1984 as a complete song. Personally, it was a trigger for my competitive instincts. Brian's early songs were far superior to mine. Academically he was far more musical. Sometimes I'd come up with a couple of chords and we'd knock them into a song together. The lyrics always came last."

Meanwhile, undaunted by a fluctuating line-up, 1984 acquired a new singer, Richard Marney, and survived for a few more years. They were content to be regarded as a solid covers group, strictly amateur with a professional bent in performance. They secured a regular spot at social functions held by Thames Television in their canteen. John Garnham, his studies over, had returned to west London and 1984, and his job with Thames Television led to this regular booking. The socials eventually became infrequent, down to just two each year by the early Seventies, and without them really noticing, 1984 had died what Dave Dilloway calls a 'natural death'. A brief claim to fame for Dave Dilloway came in 1973 when a group with whom he was playing, Amity, appeared on the television talent competition, *Opportunity Knocks*.

In 1990, the line-up of 1984 which had featured Brian May was reunited by Queen's fan club. They met at Dave Dilloway's home in Surrey and swapped stories while they sat around in the back garden. Characteristically, Brian May was half way down the front garden path before he realised he'd left his coat in the car. He told the others he had not brought along his girlfriend, Anita Dobson, because he had not wanted to turn it into a 'showbiz occasion'. Instead, he drank lager from a can, strummed his very first guitar, an Egmond, which he had swapped with Dave Dilloway many years before, and generally seemed to be much the same man they had last made close contact with nearly twenty-five years before. "He is just one of nature's nice guys," said Dave Dilloway. "I was amazed that he seemed untouched by it all. He is not the big 'I am'. He is very humble and he came to our modest semi and blended in so well. He is a very good listener. He stops and listens, unlike some people who give you the impression that they are about to rush off at any moment. He has a hell of a heart in him."

Of Poona, And Feltham

Chapter IV

Queen

Zanzibar, though it is now known by the name Tanzania, is a remote island in the Indian Ocean, nearly twenty-three miles from the east coast of Africa. The clear, blue sky has a long lifespan each day and the pace is languid. The islanders let the sun do their work. They pick the fruit, coconuts and spices, and eke out a modest living today, much like they did yesterday and the day before.

Bomi and Jer Bulsara had lived on the island all their lives and Bomi, a civil servant, worked in the early Forties as a High Court cashier with the British Government. He was based at the Beit El Ajaib, the 'House of Wonders' built by the Sultan Barghash at the end of the nineteenth century. The British Empire, of which Zanzibar was part, was contracting, but the bureaucracy of colonisation was still very much in place.

The Bulsara's first child, Farookh, was born on September 5, 1946, at the Government Hospital in Zanzibar. The island formed the perfect backdrop to a happy childhood. Farookh jumped rock pools with the other children at the beach and lost all sense of time as he played in the grand botanical gardens attached to Zanzibar museum. His father finished work at 1.30 pm each day because it was much too hot to carry on after that time; it meant there were many family outings. In their home they would inculcate Farookh with their own Persian culture, reading to him fables and legends like The Arabian Nights. Bomi Bulsara was quite well paid, and the family had servants and a relatively high standard of living.

At the age of five, Farookh moved with his parents to Bombay, India; these regular upheavals were part of Bomi's job and for a while they had lived in Pemba, another isolated island, which in the Forties had no electricity supply.

As devout followers of the Zoroastrian religion, Bombay formed the Bulsara's spiritual home. India was extremely tolerant of other religions, and Parsees (the name given to the adherents of Zoroastrianism) had fled there in vast numbers in the seventh and eighth centuries to avoid persecution by Muslims. The Parsees formed a strange social mixture. They adopted the language and dress of the Hindus, but they later acquired a peculiar 'Englishness' borrowed from the country's most recent visitors; the island had been part of the British Commonwealth since 1890. Perhaps the ceremoniousness of the English way of life and its tea-on-the-lawn civility appealed to their innate sense of pomp. It may also have been a reactionary statement directed at their host country.

While the family (now with the addition of a daughter, Kashmira, born in 1952) resided in Bombay, the world's seventh most populated city, Farookh was sent to St Peter's, an English boarding school 50 miles away in Panchgani. His school in Zanzibar had been a missionary school run by nuns, but this was a very different affair. In keeping with the colonialist tradition of imitating all things British, there was a great emphasis on etiquette. They played cricket in the sun in lily-white flannels, meals were served precisely on time, and vowels were never flat nor aitches dropped.

Panchgani is a hill town near Poona of just 3,000 inhabitants. It is far enough away from the hubbub and pollution of Bombay to give credence to the idea that it is a healthy environment in which to raise children. So healthy, in fact, that in 1957 when Farookh moved there, it had four schools, two for girls and two for boys. After taking the slow train from Bombay to Poona, the visitor takes a bus ride up into the clouds to Panchgani where there is a panorama of gentle slopes to the plain below.

On the day he first travelled to St Peter's, Farookh met four other boys also on their way there – Farang Irani, Bruce Murray, Derrick Branche, and Victory Rana, a grand name for someone of grandiose ancestry, a relation to a king no less. The five of them immediately forged friendships which would last throughout their school years.

Farookh more usually became 'Freddie' to his friends and teachers, a term of endearment his parents also adopted. They even referred to him as such in their message on his funeral wreath - 'To our very beloved son Freddie, we love you always. Mum and Dad'.

St Peter's was efficiently run, the boys given a sense of freedom and encouragement, and the tolerance shown to the different religious persuasions exceptional, though Church of England was obviously the official school faith.

"I can think of nothing ugly about the place or the time we had there," said Derrick Branche. "I recall that Freddie's and my schooldays were, if not the proverbially happiest days of our lives, then certainly a time of great joy, for in our innocence we had a marvellous time."

The school was run like a typical English public school, and Freddie took his place with about twenty other boys in the school dormitory. His first public singing was in the school choir. Its number was complemented by girls from one of the nearby schools. Indeed, one of these girls formed Freddie's first crush, Gita Bharucha.

The five boys who had met each other at Poona railway station formed themselves into a pop group and called themselves The Hectics. Freddie was a rather shy, reticent boy and was happy in the background thumping out basic chords on the piano while Bruce Murray took on the role of front man. They practised in a spare dormitory and soon became the unofficial 'school band', appearing at fêtes and school functions. Their heroes were Cliff Richard, Elvis Presley, Little Richard and Fats Domino and they belted out enthusiastic cover versions. Much of it was plain mimicry, down to the local girls screaming at the front of the stage; from half a world away they had kept a close watch on America and England.

Freddie was quiet but not afraid to express himself to either pupils or teachers. His school friends recall him 'screaming like a banshee' whenever he felt his feelings were being ignored. He was a good sportsman, excelling in table tennis and cricket. He also boxed in several competitions at the school, though his tall, lithe frame was not particularly suited to the sport.

During the holidays he would return to Bombay to be with his parents. The harbour port lying in the Arabian sea teemed with people and life and was a fascinating place for a boy to grow up. Although it was India's commercial centre, much of it remained unspoiled and unchanged from centuries earlier. He would slip into the city, past the beggars and broken-down taxis, and head for the street bazaars. Snake charmers played their strange reedy tunes, fakirs reclined on beds of nails as proof of their faith, children begged incessantly, and traders cried that their mangoes or coconuts were the best in Bombay. At the harbour, workers toiled in the sun, washing clothes, beating them dry against stone slabs, naked backs leaking sweat. And out to sea, ships set sail heavy with tea, cotton and rice.

Perhaps much of the splendour and ceremony which later became Queen's trademark was due to Freddie's involvement with the Zoroastrian religion. He often went with his parents to the fine temples to worship. Sacred fires were lit in these imposing temples and prayers said before them as an act of faith. In Iran some fires have been alight for more than two thousand years and they are tended throughout the day by priests. Freddie was inducted into the religion as an eight year old at a ceremony called Navjote. He was given a purifying bath; it is believed a clean body pre-empted a similar mind and soul. The priest chanted prayers while this took place, and afterwards in the shadow of an eternal fire, the new member repeated prayers and accepted the religion as revealed by Ahura Mazda to Zoroaster. At the end of the ceremony a sudreh, a white muslin shirt, another symbol of purity, was presented and a kusti, a cord made from lambs' wool. The kusti was wrapped around the waist three times and many Zoroastrians wore it for the rest of their lives to remind them of Ahara Mazda. The final act was to shower the initiate with coconut, pomegranate, rice and rose petals while he wore his new clothes.

Jer Bulsara was adamant that Freddie learned to play the piano and she encouraged him to take lessons at school, for which the family had to pay an additional fee. At first he did these to placate her wishes but he fell in love with the instrument and eventually attained a grade five in the examination. It equated to a bizarre musical antecedence for Freddie. In the town he would hear the florid, apparently formless drone of traditional Indian music; the cinemas were awash with expansive Indian harmony songs; the piano lessons at school were based on classics and opera; and, all the time, pop music was a growing and vigorous influence.

Despite an emphasis on sport, St Peter's was liberal enough to accommodate boys with artistic leanings. Mr Davis, the music teacher, used to hold sessions after tea in the evenings. He would play the boys pieces from operas and readings by classical English actors like Olivier and Gielgud. Freddie often appeared in school plays, most notably in *Cure For The Fidgets*. He was the 'doctor' and his characterisation included a suit, tie, heavily framed glasses and his hair swept back from his face.

"Whenever I think of Freddie at school, I always remember him smiling," said Derrick Branche. "He seemed to be perpetually smiling, and thinking of that makes me smile too."

St Peter's, in keeping with a general public school education, imbued boys with certain qualities and traits. Freddie himself acknowledged that above all else it had taught him independence, to fend for himself. It also gave him a certain conceit, an imperviousness, and it was probably an important factor in his sexual development. Statistics show that homosexuality, as far as it was ever possible to equate it with any social grouping, was more prevalent among people from single sex boarding schools. Like any tendency, homosexuality depended on availability and especially in a teenager's formative years, the all-male environment would almost inevitably have led to same-sex experimentation. Freddie showed an interest in girls, but out of necessity his adolescent happiness, sadness, sensitivity, hopes and desires were played out almost exclusively with males.

While he was at St Peter's, Freddie's parents moved back to Zanzibar. After his 'O' Levels, of which his best grades were in Art, English and History, they were reunited when he went back to Zanzibar to live in their new flat. He arrived home to the usual serenity; servants ironing his clothes, domestics helping his mother in the kitchen. It was a peaceable, uncomplicated life. Unknown to Freddie, the country was on the cusp of radical change. Britain was in the long process of disengaging its colonies and permitting countries to elect their own sovereign government. Zanzibar was comprised mainly of Africans with smaller social groupings of Arabs and Indians. In the autumn of 1963 an election was held and an Arab party came to power.

Africans in Zanzibar, many of whom assumed Zanzibar was their rightful territory because of its close proximity to the continent, were irate. They formed their own party, Afroshirasi, and assumed they would win the next election. They did not come to power at the next two hastily arranged elections and they naturally became suspicious of the balloting procedure. Nevertheless, the British Government handed over rule of the island in January 1964 to the Arab Sultan, just weeks after it had been declared an independent state.

Like much colonial business, too much had been left in abeyance and the British departure created social havoc. The Africans, exhausted by a flawed mandated system, resorted to violent means and a revolution broke out across the island. Many of the remaining British and the indigenous Indians feared for their lives and quickly left the country. The revolt eventually led to Zanzibar being united with an area on the African mainland formerly known as Tanganyika; together they became Tanzania.

The Bulsaras, carrying just two suitcases crammed with clothes and belongings, fled to England, a country on whose behalf Bomi Bulsara had served most of his life; a country they trusted and which they covertly revered, believing it to stand for decency, dignity, impeccable fair play. They contacted relatives already living in England and early in 1964 arrived at Feltham, a small town hidden on the west side of London. Falling within the county of Middlesex, and now trapped in the cheese wire grip of the M25, it is just a few miles south of Heathrow Airport, part of the ultimate urban sprawl that eases into the more sylvan, suburban charm of Sunbury, Staines, Chertsey, Walton-on-Thames and Esher. It is served by Hatton Cross tube station, which aside from Heathrow Central, is the most westerly point on the whole of London's tube system.

The contrast between Zanzibar and Feltham could not possibly have been greater. The weather was perpetually damp and overcast, the only flora was privet hedges and sycamores in the municipal park, and people went about their business in drab clothes, in the archetypal starched British manner. Freddie Bulsara was the quintessence of exotic foreignness, a unique seventeen year old, but to people living in Feltham he was another swarthy youth; he might have been a Pakistani, Bangladeshi, or from any other far away country where Britain was begrudgingly fulfilling its empiric obligations. Either way, the welcome was muted. The Bulsaras could make of England what they wanted, or go home if they didn't like it.

Freddie, who was still spending hours stabbing out paintings and drawings, decided to aim for art college. He signed up for a fashion and art course at Isleworth Polytechnic in west London. Every day he would line up with the other teenagers and travel on one of London's famous red double-decker buses to Isleworth, a small town between Hounslow and Richmond-upon-Thames. In later years Freddie rarely spoke of his early days in England and many believed it was a time of particular melancholy. The move would have certainly caused traumatic cultural confusion, and while there was no evidence of bullying, Freddie quashed his natural exuberance and hung low his head with the others at the bus stop.

The Bulsaras put down a deposit on a modest house in Feltham and Bomi found work as an accountant with one of the major employers in the area, the Forte catering company. Freddie, like many students, worked in the summer holidays, firstly in the kitchens at nearby Heathrow Airport, and then in a warehouse at Feltham Trading Estate. The other workers commented on his delicate hands and Freddie was soon using this perceived fragility to his own gain; he was excused most of the heavy work and they did it on his behalf. When the warehouse staff asked the college boy what his plans were for the future, Freddie told them he was to become a musician; this was the first time he had been overt about his dreams.

Freddie saved his earnings but announced one day to his mother that he wanted to give most of it away. She had been depositing the cash on his behalf at the Post Office and he had accumulated about £70. He told her a friend was about to be evicted from his flat and desperately needed money. He asked her to draw out £50 and when she asked if he would get it back he shrugged his shoulders. It was an early example of the generosity for which Freddie became famous. In later years such altruism came easy, it invariably did with fabulous wealth, but Jer Bulsara saw the early episode as a snapshot of his personality. "That was his way, always generous, always thoughtful of others," she explained.

After Isleworth he was accepted to study graphic illustration at Ealing College of Art and in September 1966 he moved into a rented flat in Kensington. He had to travel a few miles through London's maze of streets to reach Ealing each day, but it at least allowed him to escape Feltham and a family from which he was growing increasingly alienated.

His timing was impeccable. The year, 1966, the summer and autumn especially, was halcyon, a unique cultural explosion across the boundaries of art, music, fashion and literature. London, the famous borough of Kensington and Chelsea in particular, was its epicentre. The capital was a blank canvas, a naked body, an open stage, an empty page, and the world waited with a rare urgency to see how it would be embellished.

Ealing College of Art had a rich tradition; Pete Townshend of The Who and Ron Wood of The Faces and The Rolling Stones were former students. The course was roughly divided between illustration, graphic art and advertising. It was a progressive syllabus, focused on a multi media approach which was later adopted at most colleges. It was not, however, a premium London art college to match St Martin's, Slade, Camberwell, Hornsey or the Central College, and it is noteworthy that three of its most famous ex-students were pop musicians and not artists. While its outlook was liberal, some students felt the tutoring was too relaxed and overlooked much of the basics of graphic design. On completion, students received a diploma from Ealing but it was not an actual Diploma of Education (Dip. Ed) which most of the other colleges awarded.

Freddie, though much emphasis has often been placed on his artistic bent, was a mediocre student. He did not have the perseverance to apply himself to the humdrum of graphics, and much of his course work was ordinary. He was undisciplined and spent too many hours indulging himself; drawing fellow classmates in grainy, almost child-like detail. He had no delusions about his own work, fellow students recall him 'roaring with laughter' at his own paintings and drawings. He was, like many art students, primarily out for a good time, the scent of bohemianism more pungent than any academic inclination. He would have been better suited to a course in fine art, it was more akin to his erratic, nebulous ideas.

In 1967 Freddie, like millions of other teenagers, discovered Jimi Hendrix. He saw him as the embodiment of cool and began to dress like him, constantly drawing his portrait – the contorted face, heavy lips, headband, wire wool hair, upside down white Fender Stratocaster – the image was everywhere, filling all the available space on the walls of his flat. Freddie's entire wardrobe was based on

Hendrix, down to the tightly knotted chiffon scarves he wore in the cleft of his neck, hanging loosely down to a multicoloured silk shirt, but the attire was nothing out of the ordinary, not by London 1967 standards at least. "Freddie wasn't an outrageous flamboyant personality at all," said a fellow student at Ealing, Graham Rose. "He was as skinny as a pencil and used to wear tight jeans or crushed velvet trousers which made him even skinnier. But what he wore was no different from what we were all wearing at that time. On the whole he was a quiet guy, though he was prone to fits of giggles."

The rare times Freddie showed any streak of exhibitionism was in his impersonation of Jimi Hendrix. He would either use a T-square or ruler to represent the microphone as he ran through an animated impression, purple haze all in his brain. He was, however, generally wary of the spotlight and had an attack of stage fright at the end-of-year college fashion show. He had agreed to model an outfit comprised of a two-tone brown jacket and a shirt made of fur and plastic. He got half-way down the catwalk, stopped suddenly, and ran back to the anonymity of the curtains.

At Ealing Art College Freddie gravitated towards Tim Staffell, who was by then an established member of 1984 with Brian May. They had much in common. "I think both of us had the tendency to draw but we didn't have real artistic quality, not like the guys who turned up on the first day with brilliantly drawn portfolios and all their plans mapped out," said Staffell. "College was like a starting point for us both. It was a time of readjustment, we were two people being created in a way." Students on the same course remember Tim Staffell wearing a pair of steel toe-capped boots which he had polished with an emery cloth until they shone like chrome. Cartoon characters were then daubed on to the steel. He had a deep interest in science fiction and the work of the English nonsense poet Edward Lear.

Like Tim Staffell, Freddie Bulsara was becoming obsessive about rock music. The capital was alive with groups and venues and Freddie was anxious to take it all in. Bands and artists like The Who, Alexis Korner and Georgie Fame would appear at west of London venues like The Attic in Hounslow, the Rikky-Tik in Windsor, and such was the profusion of clubs, south west London had three top-notch venues, the Eel Pie Island Club on the Thames at Twickenham, St Mary's Ballroom in Putney and The Crown pub in Richmond, where promising new groups like Rare Bird would appear. Freddie was also a regular patron of the music club held during lunch times at Ealing College where, among the many guests, were Chicken Shack and Tyrannosaurus Rex. "I went to some of the concerts with him and after one he said to me that he too would be a pop star one day," said fellow student Gillian Green. "It was just a throw-away remark. Everyone seemed quite flamboyant back then, making outrageous statements, so it was nothing new to hear someone talk like that."

Tim Staffell, who was as close to Freddie as anyone at this time, saw few, if any, of the outrageous qualities he was to later adopt. "The Freddie Mercury Queen persona just wasn't there at Ealing," said Tim Staffell. "When I was at college I was naïve, egocentric, ignorant - and my experience since has led me to believe that so was everyone else. We were all searching for mutual growth, fencing with each other if you like. Freddie was much like everyone else, except I remember him having a more dry sense of humour. I thought he was more cynical than everyone else. He was mildly cynical at a time when people weren't cynical at all. He was not destructively so, it was a humour device."

As they progressed through the course, the students competed with each other to see who could dress the most shockingly. Freddie painted all his finger nails black and it became part of his image around college. Although he was known for his high-pitched cackle, extravagant mannerisms, and a certain epicene quality, few of his contemporaries considered him to be homosexual. David Bowie had made androgyny chic, and to a lesser extent homosexuality had been sanctioned as a valid statement of liberation. At least one other student on Freddie's fashion course had been homosexual and there would have been no real reason to hide his feelings; in fact, it might have earned him a certain kudos. "Freddie was very easy in the company of women, very matey," said Gillian Green. "I don't think he was concealing that he was gay, because I don't think he was at the time. I know of girls he went out with and I know for a fact he had a relationship of about six weeks with one of them."

He was known for his expressiveness, but most people knew him only on a superficial level. He revealed very little about himself or his background. "He was very easy going," said Gillian Green. "He had a lot of bon homie, but there was a lot he kept to himself. He was shy in many ways and used to blush quite a lot, and then get embarrassed because he was blushing." On one of the rare times he spoke of his past, Freddie eulogised life in Zanzibar to another student, John Matheson, and promised to one day take him there so he could see such beauty himself. Gillian Green found Freddie of a very different disposition on the extremely rare occasions he mentioned his past. "He talked about his background as if it was repressive and enclosed," she said. "You could tell he didn't like talking about it. He said he was so glad they had come to England. He could not understand why his parents had made so little attempt to integrate. He was a bit scathing actually, about how they could come to this country and make so little effort. He told me they could barely speak English. They seemed to want to disappear but he didn't."

Aside from the shock of a new country and culture, the Bulsaras had suffered a great blow to their dignity. In Zanzibar and India Bomi Bulsara had been a fairly high-ranking official, mixing in diplomatic circles, and with enough wealth to afford servants and pay for Freddie's privileged education At Forté's he was a down-table accountant; it was perhaps understandable that, unlike Freddie, they would pine for their former life. Through their religion and circle of Parsee friends they were attempting to build a small bastion of Zanzibar in Feltham.

Freddie's public school education precipitated his estrangement from his parents which was completed when they moved to England. There was a harmony between them again before Freddie's death, and indeed his funeral was in accordance with the Zoroastrian faith, but their relationship in life, if not death, was shallow.

Without a past, and with a family fused to the shadowy background, Freddie was able to become whatever he wished. He never spoke with Tim Staffell of his family, and Tim did not detect 'a trace of him being different or trying to find his feet.' The obsession of the times was self-discovery and Freddie capitalised on this. His parents had inadvertently left him the widest canvas imaginable; with a swish of a cloak, or feather boa, Freddie was about to devour life, and the times when he would look over his shoulder were so seldom as not to matter.

That Uncertain Smile

Chapter V

Queen

The genesis of a rock group owes much to chance, and Queen's passage was of greater convolution and implausibility than most. The core of a band is best forged in the school yard, youth club or neighbourhood, where the protagonists find others to make music with, stay friends, develop at the same pace, and share the same vision long enough to play a few concerts and ultimately make a record. The four who became Queen shared an inventory of unlikely coincidences, and this after they were denied the luxury of coming from the same neighbourhood.

Individually, they were each exemplary players who had undergone thorough apprenticeships, though Freddie's was somewhat condensed, and all four had a certain personal confidence and ambition. They were drawn together magnetically, first to London, then to one another, and it is impossible not to see their formation as uncanny at the very least. Rock music draws its very lifeblood from such splendid accidents. While it remains imprecise, impulsive, open to chance, it thrives; after that - usually by the third album - it is often moribund, waiting for the non-accident of death.

The four teenagers who later became Queen found themselves walking the sunlit streets of London or sweating in the stale heat of the Underground in the summers of 1967 and 1968. Ostensibly they were in (and around) the capital to study, and, where Brian May and John Deacon were concerned, they studied very hard indeed. But they were also seeking lives which were faster, brighter and more rewarding than those they had left behind with the tidy driveways, manicured lawns and family saloons of provincial England.

Roger Taylor began his degree in dentistry at the Royal London Hospital, Whitechapel, in October 1967. The first part of the course was devoted to pre-clinical work, and was based solely within the hospital. He moved into a flat in Sinclair Road, Shepherds Bush, in the west of London, behind Kensington Olympia; this impressed his fellow students since they mainly found lodgings in the poorer areas near the hospital in east London. Roger moved in with a friend from Truro, Les Brown, who had begun his course at Imperial College a year earlier and was already sharing his flat with two other male students.

During his first year Roger did not join a group in London, but in the summer break of 1968 he returned to Cornwall for some unfinished business. The Reaction had not wound up after the road accident, indeed they had held a meeting and categorically decided to continue, though they obviously had to break up temporarily while Roger and Michael Dudley were away at university. Incidentally, Michael Dudley had initially been offered a place at London University which would have meant he could continue playing music with Roger, but he was later accepted at Oxford and went there instead. He was to become one of a good number with valid claims that fate had frozen them out of consideration for Queen.

Roger Taylor and a good friend of his from Cornwall, Rik Evans, hatched a plan to stage itinerant concerts. Rik had started as a labourer with Penrose Marquees, a small Cornish business first established in 1840. The company, owning just six marquees, had come up for sale and Rik bought it during the mid-Sixties. He and Roger shared the same love of music, indeed Roger was a regular visitor to Rik's home where they would listen attentively to Jimi Hendrix albums. In the summer of 1968 they promoted a series of 'happenings' under canvas on the beaches throughout Cornwall. The 'Summer Coast Experience' featured a self-made psychedelic (everything in 1968 was prefixed by this adjective) light show and an appearance by The Reaction, all for the princely sum of five shillings.

Roger Taylor, with Rik Evans' assistance, was now a veritable cottage industry. Before each show he would drive around in a Mini van pasting fly posters on any available wall. Perranporth beach was popular with surfers, and they tried to make shows coincide with the finals of surf competitions. "One of our best nights was a gig at Perranporth," said Rik Evans. "The local life-saving club had a barbecue and the beach was packed out with about 500 people. We used to sell cans of Coke at the entrance to the marquee, it went down really well that night." The owner of the beach did not share their enthusiasm and was upset to see them making such healthy profits on his land; he petitioned the council to have them banned.

Other nights on the beach tour were not so successful, especially one at Trevellas Cove, just a few hundred yards down the coastline from St Agnes. The route to it was along a narrow path, through a derelict mine-working area. The chances of the area being granted permission to host such an event were less than nil, but Roger and Rik were undeterred, and scornfully worked outside the confines of proper legality anyway. It began to rain heavily and the generator packed up.

Someone trekked to the nearest house and asked for permission to plug into their electricity supply. A long trail of wire was laid down to the beach, via various plug-boards and puddles, to allow the band to switch on. Their efforts went cruelly unrewarded - only five paying customers turned up. "I have a vivid memory of this one rocker dancing on his own, splashing about in all these puddles; it was a desperate scene," said Rik Evans.

Inevitably, when Roger left Cornwall to return to London in the autumn of 1968, The Reaction drifted apart for good. Michael Dudley played chamber music at university before falling in and out of blues bands down the years. He is now an executive with the Prudential Insurance Company in London. He often ponders on how life would have progressed if his destination after leaving Truro had been London and not Oxford: "I would have been delighted to have kept up the music career. Mine and Roger's whole life was playing in those bands. That was everything to us, apart from chasing women." Rick Penrose was asked by Roger to join him in London and play music but he turned down the offer; he was married with a mortgage and needed a degree of security. Rick later joined a cabaret group called Memory Lane and has worked full-time as a musician ever since.

The summer frolics of 1968 had focused Roger, and he returned to the capital determined to form another band. Les Brown told him of a note pinned to a board at Imperial College seeking a Ginger Baker/Mitch Mitchell type drummer. Roger contacted the name on the card and within a few days received a letter from Brian May. The note was typical of Brian; precise, thoughtful and serious-minded. In unambiguous terms it outlined exactly the type of person the group required to fill their drum stool.

Tim Staffell and Brian May had adopted a radically different perspective since their days together in 1984. The distance between 1964 and 1968 was spectacular in its effect on Britain's youth. Helen Shapiro had been superseded by Julie Driscoll, Billy J. Kramer by Jim Morrison, The Shadows by Cream. The coyness and ready conformity was gone forever, and Brian May and Tim Staffell's ideology reflected these changes. Individuality was everything and in support of this free expression, their new group would write mainly their own material, or interpret others from a unique panorama. Tim Staffell had adopted the concept of a group called 'Smile' as part of a college project and built a graphics campaign around it.

Brian May was still obligated to his studies, however, and this meant his commitment to Smile was always vaguely compromised, though it was still tangibly a different undertaking from 1984. "It is fair to say there was serious intent with Smile," said Tim Staffell. "Long-haired musos were not the flavour of the month when we were around our parents and we had to keep a low profile sometimes. Brian's folk wanted him to keep on with his academic career. If we hadn't have had to keep up that façade, everyone would have seen we were really going for it."

Roger Taylor's first audition for Smile took place at his flat in Shepherd's Bush. Brian and Tim turned up with acoustic guitars, which was fitting since Roger had left his drum kit behind in Truro and had only a pair of bongos to hand. They struck up a friendship immediately, spoke the same language; of ambition, of an earnest devotion to 'good' music, and of a quiet, but perceptible assurance. They played together at volume for the first time in the Jazz Club room at Imperial College. "Roger was bloody brilliant," said Tim Staffell. "We were bowled over and were both thinking: 'This guy's great'. He was punchy and flamboyant and really showed up my bass playing."

Their personalities fused immediately and they quickly developed an innate confidence in their union. "I was always more of a vulgar kind of person than Brian," said Staffell. "Brian was laid back, a gentleman. 'Straight' is not really the right word, he was just more gentle. I was more rough around the edges as a person. My relationship with Brian was kind of gentle but when Roger turned up he was more like me, or somewhere half-way between me and Brian. Roger turned a straight line into a triangle. It created a tight self-contained unit and with it the band's own personality. Roger was lively and exciting and running on adrenaline. He was always 'up'. He was physically a drummer and also of that nature as a person. Smile were really enhanced by Roger's energy."

Their first concert was quite a scoop, supporting Pink Floyd at Imperial College on October 26, 1968. Pink Floyd had broken out of their trippy London clique with 'See Emily Play', a Syd Barrett-flavoured Top Ten hit just a few weeks before their appearance at the college; it was an auspicious start for Smile. With only a handful of their own completed songs, they resolved to re-write other people's music. Delighted to tag themselves 'progressive', it gave them a licence to drag out basic rock songs into twenty-minute jams, with numerous changes of pace and the introduction of their own bizarre chord changes, not unlike Pink Floyd in fact. They went down well, schizophrenic rock invariably did in the late Sixties.

Imperial College had a fine reputation for promoting exciting groups and Smile, as the 'in-house' band, were often given support slots. This allowed them to develop their material in front of a receptive audience and they soon became a tight, intriguing band, blending intricate vocals with rock dynamics. Since the advent of Cream and The Jimi Hendrix Experience, trios were very much in vogue, unlike a few years earlier when any group with fewer than four members was considered under powered.

Brian May had actually completed his formal degree studies at Imperial. He had received his Bachelor of Science (BSc) certificate from the Queen Mother just two days before Smile's début show in support of Pink Floyd. He continued to give tutorials at the college and worked on his PhD thesis. Staying in London also allowed him to be near his new girlfriend, Christine Mullen, a student from the Maria Assumpta Teacher Training College in Kensington whom he would eventually marry. They had met through one of Roger's girlfriends, Jo, a flatmate of Christine's, and the pair were inseparable.

Smile soon picked up two important allies. Pete Edmunds, an old school friend of Brian and Tim, became their roadie after selling his MG sports car to buy a van, and John Harris, a friend of a friend, became the sound engineer because he had a penchant for repairing amplifiers. John Harris became extremely close to the band, an invisible member in fact, as he shaped their sound from the mixing desk.

During the early part of 1969 Roger and Brian were finally introduced to Freddie Bulsara, Tim Staffell's friend from art college. Despite having once lived less than a mile from each other in Feltham, Brian May had not met Freddie until they were brought together by Tim Staffell. Freddie was liked a great deal; he was effusive, full of ideas, and in his white satin trousers he was the model of King's Road vogue. He attended rehearsals and became a regular feature in the van as they travelled to shows. He had a keen eye for the theatrical and his counsel was respected, though he was sometimes dismissed as a 'bloody nuisance' when his advice became too didactic. No one thought to ask from where Freddie's wisdom emanated, they just accepted that it was inborn. "I don't think I've ever met someone so outrageous since," said Les Brown. "He was very enthusiastic about everything, I mean amazingly so. I remember he once physically dragged me into a room and made me listen to this soul record he really liked. No one admitted to still liking soul at that time, it was all rock, so I suppose he was showing his catholic taste."

Roger Taylor contacted an old friend from Cornwall, Peter Bawden, and Smile were soon back on the live circuit already well trodden by The Reaction. "Those weekends in Cornwall were highlights of our time with Smile because everyone used to make such a great fuss of us down there," recalled Tim Staffell. "It always became a great social thing with lots of drinking sessions. It was all so much more relaxed than in London, and everyone was so kind, inviting us to their homes and to parties and so on."

Peter Bawden was a close friend of Roger Taylor and helped organise most of their escapades in Cornwall. He was eight years older than Roger with a wealth of experience in the music business. He had played guitar in The Staggerlees, a Cornish band signed to Oriole Records in the early Sixties. They had undertaken several national tours supporting early British rockers like Joe Brown, Shane Fenton and Paul Raven, later to become Gary Glitter. They folded after a road accident involving their van, following which Peter returned to Cornwall to set up Eclipse, an agency booking nationally known bands into Cornish venues. He also started PJ's Club in Truro, named after himself, Peter John Bawden. He was at the heart of the Cornish scene, and his experience of the music business was quite rare in the South West; to Roger Taylor he was irresistible. "Roger was the sort of guy, who, if he met someone as interested in music as he was, he was absolutely passionate," he said. "We used to talk about what bands to book into the club and he was always full of enthusiasm. He was different from the rest, very dedicated to the music and he never varied."

Together they organised Smile's early shows in Cornwall. Brian May sometimes stayed at Peter Bawden's house or the band would make their way back to Roger's mother's house in Truro. Peter Bawden had been an admirer of The Reaction but he felt Smile had more of an edge: "They were good, a lot of their stuff they kept on with when they became Queen. Tim was a super guy, a pretty straightforward rock singer. At the time I didn't think they were missing anything but when Freddie came along he was obviously in a different ball-park."

Roger Taylor's mother, Win, who later remarried and took the surname Hitchens, was happy to have the band stay at her house. "I always found Brian to be very sincere," she said. "He was the quiet, vegetarian type, though I don't think he actually was a vegetarian. Brian was always a bit forgetful. He turned up once without his guitar and Roger was not best pleased. Of them all, Freddie was the quietest and shyest one. He was not a conversationalist at all. His clothes were always spotlessly clean and he seemed to be able to lay his hands on a pair of white trousers at any time. He was always effeminate but we used to say, 'Oh Freddie, just get on with it'. He had longish black hair and they were all wearing fur coats at the time. They stood out a bit in Cornwall. If I was out shopping with my daughter and we saw the band we'd sometimes hurry the other way!"

Friends of Roger Taylor's from Cornwall, including Peter Bawden, would often visit him in Shepherd's Bush: "I stayed with him in his flat a few times. He hadn't changed at all. He adapted to London life as if he was born to it." Cornish parochialism was still alive and well though, as Rick Penrose discovered: "I'd left my car parked outside Roger's and when I got up in the morning there was a piece of paper under the wipers. I thought it was a parking ticket at first, but it turned out to be a letter from someone. It said something like, 'I couldn't help but notice your Cornish number plate, if you'd like a cup of tea with a fellow Cornishman, my door number is so-and-so'. I couldn't believe it!"

The Cornish contingent took to Roger's new friend, Freddie Bulsara, with sincere warmth. "I found him to be one of the genuinely nicest people I have ever met in my life," said Peter Bawden. "I remember I was walking through Kensington Market a few days after I'd first met him. I heard someone shouting my name and when I turned round it was Freddie and he just wanted to say hello. He had no need to do that, but he had made the effort. He was a delightful man in every respect." There was, however, some puzzlement as to Freddie's sexuality. "I was obviously aware of his campness, but I never saw him as homosexual," said Bawden. "To me, it was all an act. I suppose they were an unusual pair because Roger was very straight and Freddie was so effeminate. I always saw Freddie's manner as a typical London affectation. He spoke like someone in the film business."

Smile continued to support established groups in London. Early in 1969 they played shows with Tyrannosaurus Rex, Family and Yes. Many thought that Smile bore a strong similarity to Jon Anderson's symphonic rock quintet. Les Brown used to often tag along to many shows. "It was a great way to get into dances for free," he said. "I'd seen The Reaction back in Cornwall and Smile were better than them. Tim was my kind of man, really into science fiction and similar things to me. He was very serious, very intense. It took me longer to get to know Brian. I'm not sure whether I properly felt relaxed with him. I think he took the group more seriously than Tim or Roger."

The Entertainments Committee at Imperial College was asked to assemble a bill for a charity show at the Royal Albert Hall. Smile were added to the roster for the concert in aid of the National Council For The Unmarried Mother And Her Child due to take place on February 27, 1969. The trio had been rehearsing with an organ player, Chris Smith, but on the way to this prestigious show they told him they didn't feel sufficiently rehearsed with him, so he was asked to sit out the performance; he never played with them again. The bill was impressive and included Free, Joe Cocker, Spooky Tooth and The Bonzo Dog Doo-Dah Band. Smile were pleased, if surprised, to be higher on the bill than Free, who had already signed with Island Records and were rehearsing tracks for inclusion on their début album, 'Tons Of Sobs', released later that year.

The event was compèred by DJ John Peel, though he has no recollection of introducing Smile or the music they made. Smile's entrance to this grand arena was absurd. Tim Staffell's guitar lead was too short and by the time he moved forwards to the microphone it had sprung out of the amplifier and trailed on the floor. It meant there was no thundering power chord beginning and his plight was compounded by his not wearing any shoes or socks on a stage littered with splinters. They opened with a version of 'If I Were A Carpenter' and continued with their own song, 'Earth', a cover of 'Mony Mony', and an obscure blues number by

Sonny Terry and Brownie McGhee called 'See What A Fool I've Been', which was later the B-side to Queen's single, 'Seven Seas Of Rhye'. Smile were loud and brash and bluffed their way through such a lavish occasion. It was an exhilarating experience but one they knew was really well above their station.

The relative success of Smile quietly impressed Roger Taylor's fellow students at the Royal London Hospital. In his general manner they thought him nothing out of the ordinary, but his burgundy velvet suit and wilful nonchalance had not gone unnoticed. He also sat at the back of lectures and soon began to make it clear that he was disillusioned with the idea of becoming a dentist. He told them he would prefer life as a rock'n'roll star and they noticed a Smile sticker on his dental anatomy folder. "He was a very ordinary bloke," said fellow student Peter Rowan. "I know others used to watch him play gigs around London, but it wasn't a big deal or anything. It was something to fill the time. While some of the students were into bird watching, Roger had his rock'n roll thing."

The pin-up of the course was a student a couple of years older than the others called Sue Morgan. There was mild surprise when she began dating Roger. "At first I think we saw him as this country boy coming to London," said Rowan. "He was a nice bloke, too good looking for his own good though. Sue was a very attractive girl and we were surprised when he got off with her."

Roger Taylor confided in Peter that he was thinking of changing courses, perhaps to study biology at London's Queen Mary College. He was still set on a life in music, but realised he needed an alternative career plan. His apathy had not gone undetected and it was clear the tutors wanted to force the issue, and they began to single him out for special attention. Ron Fearnhead, a respected figure in dentistry and the author of a seminal paper on the structure of tooth enamel, was holding a class and began quizzing Roger. "He asked him, 'What's this?' and pointed to a bone between the eye and ear," recalls Rowan. "Roger said it was the zygoma which was correct. Ron then asked him what was the meaning of the word in Greek and Roger replied, 'Is this a dentist exam or a fucking Greek exam?' I think, after that, there was an obvious feeling that they were out to get him. He was throwing away his chance of becoming a dentist and chucking away his career I suppose. It quite impressed me in a way."

Until this point Roger Taylor had made a reasonable contribution to the course. He was one of about 40 students learning their way around the human body, concentrating mainly on the head and neck. They were split into groups of four or five and each given their own corpse to work on throughout the year. "They were this horrible black, slaty grey colour and there was this all-pervading stench of formaldehyde," said Peter Rowan. They were asked to respect the corpses, but rumours persisted of students who had carved pet names for the deceased, usually 'Joe' or 'Fred' for a man, into their torsos. Some allegedly skipped with entrails, or amputated arms to hang later from tube trains; any of this malarkey and students were threatened with expulsion.

Roger Taylor largely kept thoughts of Smile and his future to himself, and did not involve the other students in his plans, though Les Brown for one guessed that he was 'more ambitious than he let on'. Peter Rowan also saw the pop star potential in him: "It would be harder to imagine a plainer bloke, though I suppose he did look a bit like a pop star. He had a full head of hair and was skinny. Our heroes back then were bands like The Who and the Stones, I thought they were all getting on a bit and rock had had its day. I remember thinking Roger had missed the boat."

After the Royal Albert Hall performance, Smile returned to the capital's less salubrious clubs and bars, varying their live work with intermittent forays into Cornwall. Roger Taylor had earned a great deal of respect during his days with The Reaction, so the billing in the South West usually centred on his appearance - 'Roger Taylor's Smile' or, on one celebrated occasion, 'The Legendary Drummer of Cornwall, Roger Taylor And...'

In April 1969 they performed at the trendy Revolution Club in London's Mayfair and afterwards were approached by Lou Reizner, a talent scout for Mercury Records. They were flattered by Reizner's interest and signed a recording contract almost immediately. The whole deal was completed within weeks of the meeting, such was Smile's resolve to release a record. The contract, as the band recalled, was initially for one single only, but no doubt included options for Mercury to release more (on its own terms) if the single was a success; few major labels would launch a new group without holding exclusivity on an artist's first few albums.

Smile were helped in securing the deal by Peter Abbey, a friend of Roger Taylor's on the same dentistry course, who held aspirations to manage rock groups. "Peter Abbey looked at the contract and said it was pretty good," said Tim Staffell. "It must have been reasonable because it didn't turn out to be anything crippling. It was a toe in the water contract, just Mercury putting in a small amount of dough to see what happened."

Although Reizner was later to make a name for himself as a producer, most notably of Rod Stewart's first two solo albums, he introduced the band to another producer, John Anthony, and booked time at Trident Studios in St Anne's Court, off Wardour Street in Soho. The elegantly coiffeured John Anthony, like Trident itself, was to later play a large part in the destiny of Roger Taylor and Brian May. "John Anthony was a bit of a lad," says Tim Staffell. "He was a nice guy but what I'd call a music business person. He was amusing and a bit dangerous, with a small 'd'; he liked to be thought of that way. He was a leather-trousered kind of guy. In the studio he was more like a film producer, dealing with the practical logistics. There was an engineer, Pete Kelsey, and he pretty much worked the desk. You've got to remember, this was the very beginning. We were relatively naïve and suddenly exposed to the big time, blown away by it all in fact."

Smile mistakenly assumed their career would be uniformly organised now they were signed to a record deal. They were completely oblivious to the indeterminate nature of the business. After recording three songs at Trident – 'Doing Alright', 'Earth', and 'Step On Me' – they heard very little until suddenly it was announced that two of the songs would be coupled together as a single, but only for the United States. In August 1969 the Tim Staffell song, 'Earth', a fresh and tuneful slant on the pervading astronautical obsession (Tim Staffell was a self confessed 'space nut' from years earlier), was chosen as the A-side with the brisk 'Step On Me', a song written by Brian May and Tim and planned originally for 1984, on the reverse. The single release must have seemed a bizarre marketing move; any groundwork done by Smile had been in the UK, in London to be more specific, and their name meant absolutely nothing in the United States. Nevertheless, similar tactics had recently paid off for Deep Purple, whose début single 'Hush' had become a US hit well before they'd crossed the Atlantic. No such good fortune attended Smile's US début which was released without acclaim and few noticed its existence.

In a sudden change of direction, Mercury decided Smile were an 'albums band' and they were asked to record more tracks, this time at Kingsway Studios in Holborn, London. Brian and Tim had spent the summer working on new material and with producer Fritz Freyer they put three songs on to tape – the beautifully twee 'Polar Bear', a jumbled sub-Deep Purple exercise called 'Blag', and a cover version of a banal, winsome song called 'April Lady', on which Brian May sang vocals. Smile's canon of songs was reasonably strong and with a certain refined distinction, but they did not gel together well as a body of work. Mercury Records passed on the option of releasing an album, but kept the tapes in its vaults for more than two decades before releasing a Smile EP In Japan only, to satiate the demand for its curio value to Queen fans.

Smile, with laudable fortitude, resolved to find a niche as a live band. They were each notable players with an undoubted stage presence and their audiences were growing larger, albeit only by a handful at each London show. They were taken on by the Rondo booking agency in Kensington High Street which had successfully established Genesis on the live scene. Tim Staffell had done some graphics work on tickets and posters, and Rondo was pleased to reciprocate with the occasional gig.

Mercury Records had still not completely jettisoned Smile, and at the end of 1969 they staged a showcase concert at the Marquee club in Wardour Street. They were the main support to Kippington Lodge, the forerunner of Brinsley Schwartz, and an early foray onto the music scene for Nick Lowe. Smile's thirty-minute performance was tight and accomplished, but the audience was impervious. The night was intended to galvanise Smile's career, but, although unspoken at the time, it was an early catalyst in their pending dissolution.

Brian May was enjoying markedly better fortune with his academic career. By the autumn of 1969 he was absorbed in his second year of post graduate studies, concentrating solely on astro-physics. Before his second year he had been invited to join a research laboratory based at Jodrell Bank, Cheshire, run by Professor Sir Bernard Lovell. It was quite an honour since only ten students each year were asked to do either a one-year MSc or three-year PhD course at the centre. Brian rejected the offer because he wanted to study zodiacal light under Professor Jim Ring at Imperial College. The astronomical equipment which had previously been used by Brian and his colleagues in Switzerland was moved to Tenerife, on the slopes of Mount Teide, the extinct volcano which forms the island. The students lazed in the sun, swam in the sea, and still found time to write two papers based on their research which were published in the Monthly Notices of the Royal Astronomical Society.

By February 1970, with Brian May spending weeks out of the country studying in Tenerife, it was apparent that, for Tim Staffell at least, Smile had run its course. Although he was later to be portrayed as foolhardy, or at the very least unnecessarily impulsive, Tim Staffell's decision to leave Brian May and Roger Taylor was made with a cool and considered heart and mind. He did, after all, leave Smile, not Queen. Smile were a solid rock group in a floundering, ill-conceived record deal, with few friends in the music business. The machinery and personnel which would later propel Queen to stardom had barely started to fall into place. Their only real resource was the natural but raw talent of its future players, namely Brian May, Roger Taylor and, on the sidelines, their mutual friend Freddie Bulsara. This talent, of course, was later nurtured and goaded, and then promoted and sold, but no one was selling Smile, not with any intent.

In elementary terms, Tim Staffell, like thousands of musicians before and since, started to believe, quite simply, that he was in the wrong group. Through friends at college he had been introduced to black American soul music and the standard rock and blues approach of Smile suddenly seemed bland and predictable. He had also become aware of the bass and drums as a rhythm section in its own right, and the creativity of rhythm in soul music appeared limitless. "I was beginning to get a rather jaundiced view of the music we were doing and my own approach to what I was playing on the bass," he said. "It caused this sense of tension within me and I was not enjoying the direction in which we were moving. I heard James Brown and thought, 'God!' and I was drifting away from the way English bands had always made music. I was trying to assimilate that music but I had no proper bass technique. Basically, I had changed musical tracks completely."

This Page: Members of The Opposition, top to bottom: Nigel Bullen, Clive Castledine, Richard Young. The Opposition in rehearsal, with John Deacon on bass (3 pictures). Jenny Fewins. The Opposition's Go Go Dancer. Ad for The Opposition's gig in Leicester.

Opposite Page: John Deacon aged 16 (third from right), on holiday with friends. The Opposition's business card. Ad for The Opposition's gig in Leicester. John Deacon (foreground) attempts Pink Floyd style imagery with Nigel Bullen. Dave Williams, latterly The Opposition's guitarist and front man (second from right with Razzle in 1972. The Opposition's set list. John Deacon's family home in Hidcote Road.

PROGRAMME

1. You Don't Know.   2 Middle bits.
2. Going to a Go Go.   1 Middle bit.
3. Meeting over yonder.   O.K.
4. Midnight Hour   2 Middle bits
5. Heatwave   Prominent End and oooo
6. Knock on Wood.   2 Middle bits
7. Hold on I'm Coming   2 Middle bits.
8. Something You Got   2 Middle bits.
9. Six Cans   2 Middle bits.
10. Something about you   Prominent End.
11. I'll be doggone.   2 Middle s and new chord change
12. Can't Help Myself   2 Middle and Voices -
13. Dancing in the Street   O.K
14. Headline News.   Wants sorting out!!
15. Emergency 999   "   "   " !!
16. I'm Growing   O.K
17. Ride Your Pony.   O.K
18. Land of 1000 Dances   Wants sorting out
19. Key to Love   O.K

Beat Group's Van In Crash

GOSS MOORS ROAD BLOCKED

Three members of a Truro beat group, the Reaction, were detained in hospital after their van was in collision with a fish lorry near Indian Queens on Saturday. The four other members of the group were taken to the Royal Cornwall Hospital (Treliske), Truro, but were able to leave after treatment.

The group was on the way to play at a dance at Dobwalls.

For half an hour traffic was held up on the A30 at Goss Moor, while two ambulances attended the accident and firemen washed petrol from the road.

The lorry driver, Mr. Gerald Broad, of Hillcrest, Shutta Road, East Looe, was unhurt, but his vehicle, which was parked on the roadside at the time of the accident, was overturned and badly damaged.

The condition of two members, Marian Little, aged 19, of 18, Richards Crescent, Malabar, Truro, and Valerie Burrows, aged 23, of 10, Truro Vean, Truro, who are in the Royal Cornwall Hospital (Treliske), was said on Monday to be improving. Peter Gill Carey, aged 17, of Penkervis, St. Agnes, who was taken to the Royal Cornwall Hospital (Treliske), was said to be in an "only fair" condition.

BRIGHT LIGHTS, SOUR MUSIC..

THE YOUNG music makers had tried on several names for size, and none of them comfortably fitted the group.

"We had various monstrosities that I'd be too embarrassed to tell you about," says their road manager, Nic Twilley.

Then, listening to a record by Jackie Lomax, a phrase from the lyrics stuck in their mind. "We just happened to like it," says Nic. "So we borrowed it."

Which is how Sour Milk Sea comes to be washing through Highfield Parish Hall in Headington, tonight, on behalf of Shelter, the campaign for the homeless.

Local lad

Chris Dummett, the 17-year-old lead guitarist, should be able to find the place without too much trouble. He's a local, son of Michael Dummett, philosophy don at All Souls, and Ann Dummett, who used to be liaison officer with the Oxford Committee for Racial Integration.

Now he lives at Leatherhead, meeting the group six days a week for practice sessions. They all take their music very seriously, Chris, "Otherwise," says Chris, "I wouldn't be doing it for a living."

They've been professional since last June, though they knew one another for about a year before that. The only changes in their ranks have been a new drummer, and a new vocalist who arrived a couple of weeks ago.

What's new

"This will probably change our whole approach," says Chris. "We are concerned about improving our music. I don't feel we are like any other group. Our approach is based on our relationships with one another."

But what makes them different? Nic Twilley says: "They are undoubtedly better musicians than the vast majority of groups at present. They are musically extremely interesting, and still developing."

Sour Milk Sea wanted this piece to be different, too, so

I agreed to let them have their say after I'd had mine! This is what they wrote:

I never had it so good. The yoghurt pushers are here. There's a place I have been and a face I have seen today. I have said all my prayers, never answered, never cared at all. But there's a sudden change in me, I'm another person inside of me. Tomorrow I am going to see the last of the blue skies above me. Lover calling, I hear your voice, solar systems that surround you all your life, they remind me that you're really from another source of light. Lover, take me to your leader. I give you body and soul. Paul Milne (bass); Chris Dummett (lead); Bob Turell (drums); Freddie Bulsara (vocals); Rubber Gallop (second guitar); Nic Twilley (roadie); and friends SOUR MILK SEA at Highfield Parish Hall, New High Street, Headington, for Shelter, Friday, March 20, at eight. Come to understand. I grow my life in the palm of your hand.

The last time they played in Oxford—which was also the first—was at the Randolph Hotel. The atmosphere in the parish hall may be rather different. There will be a discotheque, a light show, and the Harlow Go-Gos from the secondary school at Old Marston.

Bette Jones, Shelter's Oxford secretary, says: "We're going to serve lots of milk and yoghurt! Let's hope it's not sour!

So good

(dated stamp: MAR 1970)

CHRIS DUMMETT was a public figure before he left his pram. This is him helping with mum's election campaign in North Ward 17 years ago.

Anthony Wood

This Page: Brian May (left) and Tim Staffell (right) at Hampton Grammar School, 1962. Tim Staffell. 1984 performing at Imperial College, London, December 1967; left to right: Dave Dilloway, John Garnham, Tim Staffell and Brian May.

Opposite Page: 1984 pictured at the Top Rank, Croydon, in 1967; left to right: Tim Staffell (vocals), Dave Dilloway (bass), Richard Thompson (drums), John Garnham (rhythm guitar) and Brian May (lead guitar). An article about 1984 that appeared in the *Middlesex Chronicle*, February 17, 1967. 1984 pictured at their 19 reunion at Dave Dilloway's home in Addlestone, Surrey; left to right: Dilloway, Richard Thompson, John Garnham and Brian May. Tim Staffell was detained elsewhe A flyer for Queen's appearance at the 1971 Tregye Festival of Contemporary Music, arranged - like all their early West Country shows - by Roger Taylor.

Futuristic group

WHAT will pop music be like in 1984? One group who thinks it has the answer to this question is based in Twickenham and called, of course, "1984."

The group comprises vocalist Tim Staffell, who lives in Teddington, bass man Dave Dilloway, from Whitton, lead guitar Brian (Brimi) May, from Feltham, rhythmist John Garpham, from Teddington, and drummer Richard Thompson, from Hounslow. They are all 19 years old except except John, who is 20.

I talked the other evening to the boys about the group, their ideas and their plans for the future. "The psychedelic music is certainly here to stay," said Tim. "It makes more of music than mere sound, it makes it a whole and complete art form."

On stage

The boys told me about their stage performances. Dave said: "We use everything in our act, including things like shaving foam, and plastic bricks that we throw around." Dave, as well as playing bass, also rigs lighting to the group's requirements to provide the "psychedelic experiences."

Although the group has been playing for over a year—is was founded first at Hampton Grammar School—the boys have only recently had enough experience and equipment to become serious semi-professionals.

Last month the group won an area semi-final at Croydon in a national talent search, and it is now awaiting news of the national winners, who will have the chance of a test company.

There are problems that stand in the way of success

though. Four of the group are students and in consequence they have not got unlimited time and money to give to group work. Brian stated his personal ambition as being "able to play well enough to respect ourselves," and while this sentiment is echoed by the rest of the group, it was obvious that big success is the wish of most members.

The boys show their many talents on stage. Brian made his own guitar (the product is amazing. It is in many ways superior to mass-produced instruments, and has a wiring system that Brian has built and designed). All stage electronics are handled by Dave.

New ideas are always formulating in Tim's mind, although he is keeping quiet about some which he calls "the most revolutionary."

After we had finished chatting, the boys went back to their instruments and gave vent to several numbers.

Treatments

Standards like "Heatwave," receive a very original treatment, mostly due to the sounds that Brian coaxes out of his guitar. Jazz chords and electronic sounds add feeling and nuance to numbers that are often churned out wholesale.

Using two bass drums for a fuller sound, Richard's drumming, combined with the full bass riffs of Dave and the steady work of John, provides a firm basis for experiments in sound — an opportunity which is not wasted.

Whatever does happen to pop music in 1984 I hope that of the type that is generated by "1984," one of the most forward looking groups today.

He attended several auditions while he was still a member of Smile before announcing to the other two that he was leaving. "Roger and Brian might have thought, 'This bastard has let us down,' but I don't recall it that way," he insists. "I'm the type of person who usually feels guilty about things like that but I don't remember feeling that way when I left Smile. They must have accepted my reasons. I had my own agenda by that point. I was heading towards something I really wanted to do. I really had the feeling that I was going from strength to strength."

Tim Staffell did not believe he had left a group on the cusp of stardom, or one with even a good chance of it. While he felt their music had certain qualities, he was sceptical about their chances of success. They each worked together well, but missed a pragmatic element. "We really liked playing and didn't really stop to think it through," he said. "It needed something external. We were a little self-indulgent in a way." The missing factor, as he realised later, was Freddie Bulsara. He brought with him an image ("I am a blue jeans, hole in the knee, heads down musician," - Tim Staffell); a master plan; a hardness (with a soft centre); and a self-absorption: Brian May and Roger Taylor might otherwise have skirted around the edges of triumph for ever, components of a band a notch or two above mediocrity.

The legacy of music left behind by Smile, however, should not be quickly dismissed. The handful of songs captured on tape have endured surprisingly well. In fact, many fans are incredulous as to why the Smile EP has never been given a proper global release. Mercury Records would be within its rights to do so, and would obviously garner extensive sales; some have speculated that clandestine manoeuvres have seen the material dismembered from the pre-Queen catalogue. The tracks were under-produced and digressive, but teemed with promise. Elements which were later brilliantly realised by Queen were already present – the unique sweeping vocal harmonies, the bold dynamics, and the polished impudence. It is difficult, for example, not to regard a track like 'Step On Me' as the natural precursor to 'Killer Queen', or 'Blag' to 'Brighton Rock'; they are at least cousins.

Of most poignancy is the similarity in the vocal style of Tim Staffell and Freddie Mercury. Clearly, any clique of friends with music as its touchstone will rouse some (subliminal or otherwise) stylistic mannerism, but anyone who considers Freddie's operatically-tinged voice unique should listen closely to Tim Staffell's vocal inflexion. The May/Staffell song 'Doing Alright' was included on Queen's first album and Freddie used Staffell's vocal dynamics on the track as a direct template for his own.

For some time after the release of the first Queen album, several of Tim Staffell's friends asked whether he had contributed some of the vocals. "We were all in the same peer group, so there might have been some copying, but my hackles rise at the suggestion that I might have borrowed from Freddie," he says. "I was always very aware of what I was doing with my voice and how I sung." Regardless of any dissent over similarity of technique, it is apparent that if Freddie was to provide the foreground to the outfit which became Queen, the background had already been colourfully painted by Smile. Tim Staffell, incidentally, has had remuneration for his part-contribution to 'Doing All Right'; down the years he estimates he has received up to £20,000 in royalties. There has never been any question of Queen eschewing their financial obligations to him.

Tim Staffell joined Humpy Bong, a group formed by Colin Petersen, the drummer who had played on the first six albums by The Bee Gees. Petersen had been a television star in Australia during his childhood when he played the mischievous scamp, 'Smilie'. Humpy Bong was basically a front for the management aspirations of Petersen and his wife. They hand-picked the group and attempted to shape it into a bubbly hit machine. Their atrocious name was taken from an Australian town, allegedly one of the first to be discovered on the Australasia sub-continent. Within a month or so of leaving Smile, Staffell appeared on *Top Of The Pops* to mime to the band's one and only single, 'Don't You Be Too Long'. Though Tim Staffell must have been unaware at the time, Humpy Bong were even further away from the music he really wanted to make. Their lively but superficial honky-tonk pop was a good deal more indistinct than Smile's and the band fell apart within a few months.

Tim Staffell later played with the English folk singer Jonathan Kelly, whom he considered the largest single influence on his life. They had been initially brought together by Petersen in Humpy Bong. After another appearance on *Top Of The Pops*, his work with Kelly came to an abrupt end when Kelly left music to become a

Jehovah's Witness. Staffell moved on to Morgan, a quartet led by former Mott The Hoople organist Morgan Fisher, which recorded for RCA in the mid-Seventies, playing what he describes as: 'keyboard based, strange, contrived music.' He finally left music in the late Seventies to concentrate on a flourishing business as a freelance animator and model maker.

Tim Staffell has always slept easily on his decision to opt out of his collaboration with Brian May and Roger Taylor. "I have never regretted it," he said. "I have regretted not being a musician, but not leaving Smile. It was good that I got out of the way because otherwise Queen would not have existed and the world would have lost a whole bunch of quality music. Smile wouldn't have done it."

Mercury Records was left with a band that had lost its singer and main songwriter and whose guitarist was living sporadically out of the country, so it was no surprise that Smile were released officially from their contract in the spring of 1970; this had already happened in practical terms a few months earlier.

The Messenger Of The Gods

Chapter VI

Queen

While Smile had been earning respect for their earnest, committed, and promising endeavour, Freddie Bulsara was still very much the dilettante. In the summer of 1969 he left Ealing College of Art with a diploma his work only just merited. During the last year of the course the idea of joining a group had become fixed in his mind. He bought a cheap electric guitar and Tim Staffell taught him the rudiments of playing. Freddie strummed out chords as a rough backing to the vocal melodies passing through his head. Unlike the other members of Queen, Freddie's musical development was brief, telescoped into just a few short years. He lived life at full tilt, too brisk for the insufferable torpor of the next church hall gig and a two-line advertisement in the local paper.

Freddie's first proper group was Ibex which he joined immediately his course had finished in the summer of 1969. Ibex had moved to London from their native Liverpool in the belief that a change of location to the home of the music business would bring them some luck. The farthest they had travelled thus far had been to appear at the Twisted Wheel club in Manchester and their press 'kit' comprised of one cutting, a snippet from the *Widnes Weekly News* about them sending a tape to Apple Records and hoping The Beatles would single out a fellow Liverpool band for stardom. This was at the time when The Beatles had promoted Apple as some kind of anti-establishment rock utopia, and even suggested that all who sent in tapes would achieve certain fame, perhaps even commiserate with their own. Somewhat predictably, cassettes, manuscripts, paintings, films, all manner of artistic outpouring from the nation's youth, arrived by the van load three times a day, piling up in sacks in their overcrowded offices in Savile Row. Ibex didn't get a response.

They were a trio comprised of guitarist Mike Bersin, bassist/vocalist John 'Tupp' Taylor, and drummer Mike 'Miffer' Smith. They had arrived in town with a close friend elevated to managerial status, Ken Testi, a 'mover and shaker', on Liverpool's music scene. "Ibex were a local response to the popularity of groups like Cream, Free and John Mayall's Bluesbreakers," said Testi. "At the time virtuoso ability was coming into fashion. We had moved on from The Beatles' format. I was very keen to help these chaps who I admired greatly. I never really wanted to play myself, I wanted to be near the music, but I never actually used the term of manager."

Unknown to Freddie (as if he cared!) Ibex had gone through the usual complex machinations of personnel before he joined them. Ken Testi had been in the same class as the group members at Wade Deacon Grammar School for Boys in Widnes. In their first incarnation they were known as Colour, a five-piece containing Mike Bersin and John Taylor along with Gordon Fraser (guitar), Ken Hart (drums) and Colin McDonnell (vocals). The advent of progressive music had a catastrophic effect on the music scene at the end of 1966 and many were cut off by the tide. Colin McDonnell, still wearing a neat shirt and cravat, was asked to leave Colour. The situation had grown so venomous that the rest of the band were hissing 'Tommy Steele' at him behind his back. The remaining members amalgamated with two singers from another Widnes band, Paul Snee and Johnny Cannon. These were a few years older and married, and within a few months had to leave to spend more time with their wives and children.

Colour later became Ibex, although Gordon Fraser's tenure with the new group was short. Gordon, standing at six feet three inches tall by the age of thirteen, was prodigiously talented, both on guitar and as a painter. Unfortunately, his enigmatic disposition was increasingly difficult to properly channel into the group and he soon left. Mike Bersin, who had hitherto mainly played electric organ, moved to guitar and a local milkman-cum-drummer, Mike Smith, replaced Ken Hart on drums. It was Mike Smith who suggested the name Ibex. At the time he was unaware that it was the name of a wild goat, but thought it sounded cool and appropriately Dadaist. Like many young people at the time, he had adopted the anarchic Dada art movement of 1915-20 as the natural brethren of progressive rock.

Ibex were ahead of their time in Liverpool which was still gripped by the amiable, simplistic meter of Merseybeat and Tamla Motown. "They wanted us to play Irish music or country and western," said John Taylor. "They didn't want us lot, bedraggled and wearing fur coats, playing 'Hey Joe'. We used to end up playing songs like 'Green Green Grass Of Home' just to keep them happy." The band made friends with Robbie Savva, a local guru of electronics. He invented a device which would allow sound to be passed from speaker to speaker in rotation. Pink Floyd were later to call the gadget an 'Azimuth Co-ordinator' but Ibex, along with Robbie Savva and his various fuzz boxes, were making outlandish noises in pubs and clubs on Merseyside without any notice. In fact, they discovered that other local bands, like The Microbes, formed by some fellow ex-pupils of Wade Deacon, were faring much better in suits, ties and presenting opportune soul revues.

London beckoned and in Ken Testi Ibex had someone with the forte to make it happen. He had already set himself up as a teenage promoter, organising several dances while still at school. He knew his way around the dark corridors and fluorescent lit offices of clubs like The Cavern where Billy Butler played records wearing his Sgt Pepper suit and the galvanising force of The Beatles was still fuel to dreams. "Ken was great," said John Taylor. "He was always a nice guy, quite sharp and always well organised. He had an eye for most things and was a good promoter."

Ken Testi had passed his driving test before the others and it fell upon him to drive their battered van – MOT tests had not yet been introduced, but Robbie Savva had primed the engine – to London. Ken's girlfriend, Helen McConnell, had moved to London to study and she put up Ken and Mike Smith at her rented house in Sinclair Road, Shepherd's Bush. Her sister, Pat, was a student at the Maria Assumpta College and she offered room space to Mike Bersin and John Taylor at her flat in Batoum Gardens, just off Shepherd's Bush Road. Ken, then aged seventeen, had only been to London twice before, firstly to see Fleetwood Mac play at a hotel in Croydon and he also hitched down for Cream's farewell concert at the Royal Albert Hall. "We were very naïve I suppose," he reflects. "We were just four lads buying a ticket for the summer. We thought we might end up as pop stars, or we'd go back home at the end and go to college. We were explorers, and there were a lot of them about in the late Sixties. It was all very Dick Whittington."

The group often expanded when Geoff Higgins travelled down from Liverpool to appear with them. He would play the bass guitar when John Taylor picked up the flute. John had 'borrowed' the flute some time before from the music room at school. Mike Bersin was the leader of the group, but John Taylor, despite being the least skilled player, provided much of the group's character. Geoff Higgins had made his début with them a few months before at the Cavern and Taylor's introduction to the débutante was hardly understated. "It was my first ever gig, at the Cavern of all places, and my legs were shaking," said Geoff. "He announced me as Geoff Higgins, who needed no introduction, as if I was famous. He was a complete head-the-ball, he just didn't care."

Ibex opened their live set with Sonny Boy Williams' 'Help Me' and the rest of the material was either blues covers or their own renditions of Jethro Tull songs like 'Waltz For A Cuckoo' or 'Bach's Bouree'. Mike Bersin had a strong distaste for Beatles' songs and was adamant that they would not include any in their set. Ironically, when Mike later became a friend of Freddie, one of the first songs they played together was a cover of The Beatles' 'Rain'. Ibex were a cheerful, easy-going bunch, happy to fall into situations. One night, while still back home in Liverpool, they travelled in their van to see Howlin' Wolf appear at the Free Trade Hall in Manchester. They did not have tickets but when the security staff saw a van full of young people draw up, they thought they were either the support group or part of the sound crew, and they were waved to the back of the venue and escorted to the stage. The members of Ibex spent the rest of the night in the wings watching a blues legend from extremely close quarters.

On the first day in London they parked their van by a phone box. Address book in hand, Ken Testi began to ring around people in the music business. The band pressed their faces to the glass, anxious to listen.

"Hello, is Chris Ellis there please?"

"This is Chrysalis. Can I help?"

Concerts were difficult to secure and apart from an audition at the 100 Club in Oxford Street and a couple of shows in Richmond, their diary was almost empty. In fact, two dates Ken had arranged before he left for London, both in the Lancashire town of Bolton, were the only immediate shows of note.

Ibex's timing had been wretched; the student venues had closed down for the summer and much of London's youthful population had returned home for the holiday. "It was a summer of getting knocked back," says Testi. "It fast became quite difficult. The sisters' neighbours were starting to get uneasy when underpants appeared on the washing line and their landlords were becoming suspicious."

A rare propitious night came at the celebrations for Pat McConnell's birthday. She had earlier seen a band called Smile perform at Imperial College and was smitten by their good looks, especially those of their drummer, Roger Taylor. She persuaded the set of friends that her birthday drink should be in The Kensington, a pub just off Holland Park Road. She knew that Smile and their friends often drank there and was keen to engineer a meeting. The two groups could not have been more dissimilar. Ibex were in scruffy jeans and T-shirts, while Roger, Brian, Tim and Freddie were in their fineries, silk scarves and fur coats. "To a degree we were the archetypal hicks from the sticks, but music, like love, conquers all," said Ken. "We had a dialogue straight away through our love of music. We were all a bit rough and ready but they weren't cocky with us at all."

At closing time they all headed for Pat McConnell's flat where Brian May picked up Mike Bersin's guitar and amazed him with his playing. Smile had been recording demos at Trident Studios and played Ibex the work in progress. "They just played a few tracks," recalls Testi. "They were very, very impressive. The vocals were absolutely brilliant and there was no doubt in my mind that I was in the presence of something very, very special. It really was blisteringly good." Freddie, incidentally, already knew the songs intimately and was harmonising with Tim Staffell's recorded voice as they lounged around the flat.

Without a distinct role in Smile beyond that of advisor, Freddie began tagging along with Ibex, proffering advice as to how the sound could be enhanced, how the stage show could have more impact. The band were all reasonable players but had few ideas about visual presentation and none of them enjoyed singing particularly; it was clear that Freddie would be invited to audition. They 'auditioned' him in the music room at Imperial College and it was with a certain inevitability that he became their new singer.

Freddie was now living with Tim Staffell, Brian May and Roger Taylor at a rented house in Ferry Road, Barnes. The members of Ibex were regular visitors and the ground floor they occupied became an impromptu drop-in centre. Geoff Higgins met Freddie for the first time when he woke up, still considerably stoned, on the chaise longe. "I was totally out of it," he recalls. "There had been a howling gale outside and Freddie walked past me and over to the mirror above the mantelpiece.

He just announced to the mirror, 'Oh God, I haven't been out looking like this, have I?' I couldn't believe it."

Ibex rehearsed frequently at Imperial College and Freddie dedicated himself to the group. Their set was now composed of incompatible cover versions by artists like The Beatles, Yes and Rod Stewart. Their opening song was a cover of Elvis Presley's 'Jailhouse Rock' which Queen later adopted for their own live shows. It allowed Freddie to indulge in gleeful histrionics, but for some time the rest of the group were unsure about Freddie's stage antics. "He used to ponce around and he was really embarrassing," Higgins stresses. "We were begging him, saying, 'Freddie, would you please stand still?' but, boy, were we wrong and was he right."

The general trend was towards a rather more staid, po-faced delivery, but their appeals for Freddie to turn down the energy went unheeded. "There was a massive cultural difference between Freddie and the others," said Testi. "He was very fashionable and particular about his appearance. The most amusing relationship was between Freddie and Mick Smith. Mick was a milkman from Widnes, as rough as a bear's arse and well-built with it. Freddie was this very nice scholar type chap with a much slighter build. They became very good friends but they took the piss out of each other mercilessly. Freddie could be quite raucous at times but generally he opened our eyes both musically and artistically. He made a massive impression on all of us, even to this day."

The shows in Bolton were to prove the high point of the summer for Ibex. Richard Thompson, Brian May's old friend from 1984, was working for an air freight company at Heathrow Airport and managed to 'loan' a new Transit van in which Ibex could travel north. John Taylor had found work at a record shop near Piccadilly Circus which stayed open until the last hippie had fallen asleep on the pavement outside and they had run out of tracks to set the turntable spinning. John Taylor's shift did not finish until midnight so they left the capital soon afterwards.

The journey to Bolton did not take as long as expected and on arrival Ken Testi was to see a juxtaposition of style and image which he would remember for the rest of his life. Freddie clambered out of the van wearing a cut-off granddad shirt, fur cape, Victorian scarf and satin trousers. As this peacock arranged his clothes on the pavement, a crew of workers finishing a night shift streamed by in their dirty, grey overalls.

The 'tour' of Bolton began on Saturday, August 23, at the recently built Octagon Theatre in the centre of the town. The concert was held at lunch time, arranged on the lines of an arts workshop. It was apparent that Freddie had improved the band dramatically. Their performance was slick and Freddie covered every inch of the stage. "There were only a handful of people there, but Freddie was immediately 'there' the minute he walked on stage," said John Taylor. "His presentation was great, visually amazing. He'd been striking these poses at rehearsal but this was great. I was genuinely stunned by him. His voice was a bit rough, but that didn't matter too much at the time."

The next show was at an open air festival in Bolton's Queen's Park. While Freddie, his body still poured into skeletal white satin trousers, was the focus of attention, his mode of apparel had influenced the rest, including even the stoical Mike Bersin who had taken the stage in a gold lame cloak made specially for him by his mother. Relations in the band were generally fine, but there were some disagreements and they saw evidence of Freddie's forceful nature. "We rowed a few times but it never got too bad," said John Taylor. "He was always strong and could hold his own. He was certainly very determined. I remember, when Queen properly got going, they used to have flaming rows. I thought that all of them had that bit of steel that it takes. There would always come a point where they would lay it on the line."

Freddie was already revealing tendencies towards pretension in Ibex. At a concert at St Helen's Technical College he ordered a lackey to find him a full-length mirror so he could properly adjust his trousers. The 'dressing room' was actually the college kitchen but Freddie held no truck with such downbeat reality. He spent half an hour tampering with his velvet trousers before taking the stage. Freddie wore his trousers so tight that it was almost impossible for him to sit down while wearing them. Several friends often caught him taking furtive glances around the room before he would quickly zip down the fly to allow him to bend down without bursting the seams.

The curious dichotomy between Freddie Bulsara on stage and off stage was already apparent to the other members of Ibex. On the boards, even the secondary ones they were treading, Freddie's persona was grand, his gestures lavish and drawn strongly like a cartoon in marker pen. He held the stage as his own, territorially, with a majestic sense of confidence. Backstage, in the broom cupboard and kitchen dressing rooms, he was small again, often smaller than the rest of Ibex. His fringe was used to hide his eyes, he covered his protruding teeth with his hand when he smiled. He would speak to the well-wishers drawn magnetically to the band, but he didn't have much to say and his voice was sometimes barely above a whisper. Occasionally, though, he was a scaled down version of his stage self, itchy, impatient, loaded with ideas. "He was a very 'up' person and a very funny character," said John Taylor. "He was always very interested in people and often turned up with quite exotic types in his company."

Josephine Ranken, a friend of Freddie's whom he had met at art college, was invited to travel to Widnes with the band. An eccentric girl, out-size in every aspect, she had her own idiosyncratic sense of style which ran to wearing bright purple lipstick. She knew dope dealers with monikers like 'The Strangler' and sometimes dressed like the principal boy in a pantomime. She was typical of the characters Freddie seemed to 'collect' during his lifetime; she was different, and gave as good as she got. "I thought I was in for a time of mad glamour but I spent the night sleeping on this floor in Widnes," she recalled. "I remember waking up, opening the curtains and staring across to a chemical works."

Josephine soon detected that Freddie was uncertain of his sexuality. His relationships with girls tended to be brief, and Josephine was privy to some gossip about his liaison with a beautiful girl on the same course, Rosemary Pearson. "As far as I know they slept together just once, but I heard, not to put it too crudely, that he couldn't get it up," she said. "He thought he liked women but it took him quite a while to realise he was gay."

She noticed that Freddie would often speak about homosexuals; they clearly fascinated him, though he never revealed that he might be attracted to men. On one occasion she invited him along to visit a homosexual friend with the pet name of 'Pixie'. They travelled together to Acton in west London with some cream cakes to share with Pixie, a handsome lecturer in his early thirties. Josephine was neither match-making nor 'testing' Freddie, it was simply a trip to visit someone whose company she enjoyed. She was shocked by Freddie's response when they arrived at the house. "Pixie was a very nice queer – we didn't use the word 'gay' in those days – really fun to be with," she said. "He certainly didn't make any advances to Freddie but he was only there a short time before he fled. He had wanted to meet Pixie but I don't think he could face up to the feelings it caused inside him. He was obviously terribly interested in homosexuality but was afraid of it as well. I suppose he was squeamish and frightened of accepting himself as gay."

Freddie's interest led him to make regular visits to a gay household near to where he lived in Barnes. He was not open with friends about his interest in homosexuality, indeed it would have been difficult for him to articulate feelings he could not properly interpret himself. He wrote a letter to a friend at this time and protested that someone had referred to him as a 'fully-fledged queer'. At this stage he was learning the parlance of being gay, its nuances, codes, ethics, its carnality and spirituality. He could excuse this interest as the dalliance of a liberal mind, drawing in the multiplicity of existence; a hazy, meaningless description for a state of being which, like music, later became a lifeblood.

Friends from this period found Freddie 'fun to be with' and recognised his unusual charm, but he was also self-centred and egotistical. "He could be quite petulant, he certainly sulked quite a lot," said Josephine Ranken. "He was not a particularly intelligent person, he was frivolous and rather silly, not someone of great profundity. You had the feeling that he wanted to be famous but wasn't really sure how to go about it. He was certainly in the wrong place at art school, his work was pretty poor."

Freddie was clearly extremely ambitious and unlike many of his peers he refused to fall into a drink or dope stupor, in fact he rarely smoked pot and was content to sip the odd glass of port and lemon. His aspiration was evident and several acquaintances suspected that beneath his dandy persona was a shrewd, unusually cool business mind. He did not have the kind of aptitude that could be applied indiscriminately, it had to be on his own terms, but there was definite focus; given the backers and the breaks he would not flounder. "He was not unpleasant, he wouldn't have climbed on anybody to get to where he wanted to be," said another college friend, John Matheson. "He certainly wasn't ruthless. I was glad when he went on to make it because there were other people from college who have done extremely well and they were much, much worse than Freddie."

Mike Bersin was astonished by Freddie's vanity; not a minute passed without him adjusting some item of clothing or rearranging his hair: "He really seemed to understand that to get somewhere, to be a star I suppose, that you had to look right. He was so conscious of his image, it was unbelievable. I suppose he was just very determined." He found Freddie's personality to be a mixture of piercing, sometimes crude melodrama, and, alternatively, thoughtful gentility: "He could be incredibly helpful at times, a real gentle guy. It depended on what mode of behaviour he happened to be in at the time."

Freddie's dalliance in music allowed him to conceal further his ethnic background. He had already reinvented himself during his passage through art college, but he was anxious to lose his surname which was too much of a clue. He suddenly announced that he wished to be known as Freddie Mercury. It seemed as if Farookh Bulsara had never really existed. Calling himself after the messenger of the gods was a move of incredible pretension, but it was done with just enough knowing irony for the others to accept it as typically Freddie.

After Freddie left his flat in Kensington to move in with the others in Barnes he got on particularly well with Roger Taylor, and in the summer of 1969 they took over a stall at Kensington Market where they sold odd pieces of art and antiques they had acquired chiefly from friends. Like most aspiring musicians they needed to earn money to cover their rent and food and the market provided relatively easy cash. They paid £10 per week to rent the stall and relished the banter and barter with the stall holders, many of whom were themselves aspiring artists, singers, writers or actors.

The pair did not really have any experience in trading in antiques, or even junk, which was how most of their friends described their wares, so they decided instead to sell second hand clothes. The market was quite chic - Julie Christie was occasionally spotted perusing the stalls and Steve Howe of Yes was a regular customer. More usually, greenhorns from out of town and tourists desperate for a slice of hip London walked the aisles and they were often willing to pay inflated prices for clothes they could have bought for a fraction of the price at a local jumble sale. Freddie and Roger, both frivolous clothes horses ("Roger and I go poncing and ultrablagging just about everywhere and lately we've being termed as a couple of queens," wrote Freddie to a friend at about this time) and instinctively knew which items to stock; they had previously been convincing fashion victims themselves. On one occasion they bought a hundred fur coats from a rag merchant in Battersea for £50 and later sold them for up to £8 each.

Their stall, though much mythologised, was extremely small. Some of their friends referred to it as 'the telephone box', though, with more than a tinge of irony, Freddie and Roger described themselves as gentlemen's outfitters. The quiet periods of the day were enlivened by the use of a devious periscope device they had set up near the till area which offered a revealing view of girls changing into mini-skirts, halter-neck tops and knee-length boots at the side of a stall opposite theirs.

The semi-detached house where they lived in Ferry Road was called 'Carmel' and it quickly became notorious among their friends. It was little more than a squat where friends could meet, lounge on any one of the mattresses scattered around, and smoke reefers. It had previously been home to people of quite different tastes - the garden was floodlit by green fluorescent lights and everything, from the ornate name sign on the wall to the cheap nylon curtains, was a model of kitsch. There was never any food in the cupboards, only tea bags and milk in the fridge, and a large dustbin was left in the middle of the kitchen floor. When the smell became too hideous to bear, the least stoned resident would drag it into the yard. At any given time it was almost impossible to discern who was paying the rent or passing through.

The occupants drank jasmine tea, smoked a great deal of marijuana, ate hash cakes and sometimes strummed an acoustic guitar propped against the wall. The dope was hidden in the jasmine tea and each week someone was allotted the job of separating the different leaves. Freddie, who usually refused to take any kind of drug, became accidentally stoned one night when he drank the 'tea' before it had been sifted. He was not sanctimonious about his antipathy to drugs and let the others do as they wished without comment. They had adopted the posture of bohemianism, but it was idealistic and indulgent rather than polemic or heartfelt. They were mostly from sheltered bourgeois backgrounds, dropping out, slumming it, treading water before turning into their parents, or superior versions if possible. Acid and wine were cheap and sex still a source of recreation. Much of the politicised conviction of the Sixties had become dissipated and only the hedonism, a rather weary version at that, remained.

Fran Leslie, another student at Ealing, felt this aura of hedonism in decline was best captured in Malcolm Bradbury's book *The History Man*. "It all got terribly romanticised afterwards but at the time it was about stealing money from friends to buy dope, regular trips to the clap clinic, Yoko Ono doing daft things at Covent Garden," she said. "The lecturers all thought the female students were perks of the job, to pick up at will. There were a few intellectuals, I remember meeting Derek Jarmen at about this time and sensing his dynamism, but otherwise everyone was young and confused I suppose. They were good times though, I'd go back there any day if I could."

Fran Leslie was on the same course at Ealing but started two years after Freddie. She remembers him calling in to see old friends and he once entered a lecture part-way through. The lecturer, Jack Drew, who was infamous for his appalling memory, ticked Freddie off.

"Do you know how late you are?" he asked.

"Yes, two years," replied Freddie.

Freddie had a unique quality which the other students weren't slow to recognise; he was rarely mocked or ridiculed for his effeminate mannerisms. "He had a slight lisp and a slightly sibilant tone to his voice," recalls Fran Leslie. "He was liked because he was friendly and gregarious. He looked very Asian with his jet black hair and dark skin. I don't recall him as being all that thin, he was quite big. Maybe it appeared that way because he was always with Roger who was very slight. They complemented each other well, Freddie dark and Roger fair. I always liked Roger. He was engaging, a sweet character with a slightly shy manner which was quite attractive."

Around this time Freddie began a relationship with Mary Austin, the woman who was to become his lifelong companion. They met during one of Freddie's frequent visits to Biba, London's ultimate fashion house based in Kensington High Street. The store was scented by incense and decorated by ferns, the sales assistants wore lilac lipstick and brightly coloured tights. Mary Austin worked there as a manageress and knew many of Freddie's circle of friends. Although it was ostensibly a boutique for women, many men also shopped there since the accepted boundaries of dress had become so indistinct. Freddie termed himself a 'Biba freak' and bought a good deal of his extravagant clothes from there; it was not surprising that his first proper relationship should be forged in such a cosmopolitan environment.

The pair had met at a time when Freddie's sexuality was at its most ambiguous. He was certainly exploring his homosexual tendencies but somehow he and Mary established a framework for a successful liaison. They were accepted as a 'couple' by their friends and were exactly that in terms of their compatibility and fondness for one another. "I know a lot of people find it hard to understand our relationship and, yes, it is an odd bond, but other people who come into our lives just have to accept it," Freddie once said. "We love each other very much and look after each other."

How Regal It Sounds

Chapter VII

The plan had always been for Ibex to spend just the summer of 1969 in London, so, once the money and enthusiasm had run out, they returned to Liverpool. Mike Smith was the first to head north. He was a few years older than the others and was offered a job as part of a construction team building the M56 which passed through Cheshire from Manchester to Liverpool. He needed the regular money so he reluctantly told the group he was leaving. He was replaced by Richard Thompson who had already learned most of the songs through attending their shows. Richard and Freddie had become fairly close friends, they lived near to one another and had similar tastes in music. One of their regular haunts was The Marquee, and Richard often drove there with Freddie singing along loudly to the radio.

Mike Bersin, always the most pragmatic member of Ibex, took up a place at art college in Liverpool, as he had promised his parents he would do if the group hadn't landed a record deal by the end of the summer. John Taylor was the only one to remain in London; he had settled into his new life and was being asked to play with other bands that congregated at the record shop.

Like many groups, Ibex's demise came about in stuttered fashion. On their return to Liverpool they were able to make contact with allies old and new through Mike Bersin's college course. They were offered gigs and Ken Testi had the onerous task of welding together a band whose members lived nearly 200 miles apart. He was keen, unusually so, and on one occasion hitched to London and back to collect Freddie. The singer responded to this determination and spent a few weeks living in Liverpool, giving it one last shot. "It was really weird seeing him around Liverpool," said Geoff Higgins. "He dressed like an alien compared to everyone else. He was always in his velvet trousers and three-quarters length coat. He had this habit of hiding his buck teeth with his top lip, pulling the lip down over his teeth somehow."

By this point Freddie had instigated a new name for the group. He had never been enamoured of Ibex, so he rang each of them, telling each one the others were in favour of a change and suggested Wreckage as an alternative. "He rang me and said the other two were up for it, so I might as well be too," said Mike Bersin. "It was so like Freddie to do that sort of thing. He was very direct and usually got his own way. We didn't really care all that much what we were called, so it didn't make much difference. I turned up for the next rehearsal and everything had Wreckage sprayed on it."

Freddie moved in with Geoff Higgins' family in the pub they were running, Dovedale Towers, in Penny Lane. He had to spend most nights on the floor in Geoff's bedroom and his tolerance of such primitive living was a testimony to his conviction to succeed. He was a good house guest and Geoff's mother, Ruth Higgins, was fond of him. "My mother liked him because he spoke properly, because he was from the South," he said. "She was glad I'd started to meet people who could speak properly. Freddie was very, very kind to her." At such close quarters, Geoff saw no evidence of any homosexual leanings from Freddie, and says he 'didn't have the slightest inkling' that he might be gay and often saw him in the company of girls. John Taylor christened Freddie 'the old queen', but he too did not consider him to be gay.

Wreckage, to Freddie, clearly had qualities which most others missed; even Mike Bersin considered themselves 'small beer' on the Liverpool scene, while Richard Thompson said they were 'rough around the edges'. They continued playing a series of poorly attended shows in the Liverpool area, appearing at clubs like The Sink, a dingy venue beneath the Rumbling Tum club in Hardman Street. The fees were low, usually about £25, of which up to £15 would be needed to cover the cost of the lights. Like many bands, their light show was at least as important as the music, and they used hot oil to create kaleidoscopic images while they played. The other members of Wreckage would have been happy to scale down the lights to leave themselves more money for beer, but Freddie was adamant that the show look professional. Freddie himself made no compromise to the size or state of the venues, or the number of people in attendance. "He gave the same kind of performances he did at the peak of his career," said Ken Testi. "He was a star before he was a star, if you know what I mean. He'd strut around the stage like a proud peacock."

Freddie did not eschew the mundane duties of life in a group. He was willing to load the van, albeit at a slower pace than the rest, and despite his manifest difference in demeanour from the others, he was not regarded particularly as an outsider. They enjoyed his enthusiasm and he was one of only a few people who ever really cared. Sometimes fellow hipsters from London would arrive to see Freddie, including Roger Taylor and Brian May, and they made an arresting sight as they cruised the streets in their velvet and satin. Glam rock, as it became tagged, had already evolved organically from hippy chic in London, but it was still filtering through to the provinces. It was during one of their trips to Liverpool when Brian, Roger and Freddie first appeared on stage together. At a show at The Sink, Freddie invited them on to the stage to jam with Wreckage and they duly obliged.

There is some confusion as to whether Freddie Mercury began writing songs in earnest during this period. Mike Bersin, who would have been his most likely collaborator, remembers only a handful of completed songs. Among scraps of ideas they worked on, he feels these may later have evolved into fully fledged Queen songs like 'Liar', 'Seven Seas Of Rhye', 'Jesus' and 'Stone Cold Crazy'. Richard Thompson, who took on the role of band archivist for Wreckage, believes it was a much more fertile period. He recalls Freddie and Mike writing between ten and twenty songs, and that most of them found their way into the band's set. "They were very melodic," he said. "Freddie had written them on the piano, I suppose it was classical piano in style. It was dead original, definitely going towards what Queen became. Freddie had so many influences, both in art and music."

Wreckage, as befits their name, soon began to fall apart for a final time. Their farewell to a music business which hadn't really noticed their existence was at Wade Deacon Grammar School for Girls in Widnes. The concert was a debacle as they struggled against a poor sound with equipment breaking down all around them, but by accident Freddie stumbled upon something which later became a Queen trademark. He was attempting to hoist a microphone stand above his head when it broke away from its base. Without its heavy 'anchor' Freddie was free to use the stand like a cane and he swirled it around, dropping it to his midriff when he wanted to mime a guitar solo. In front of a few dozen girls in Widnes it seemed a rather witless, meaningless act, but, mainly through Live Aid, it later became an indelible rock'n'roll image, like Paul McCartney's violin bass or Mick Jagger's elastic lips.

"It wasn't all that sad that we split up, we hadn't done that much together," said Richard Thompson. "I still saw Freddie around as a friend. It was obvious at this point that Freddie was keen to make it because he was more or less running the band at the end." The drummer moved to the United States and on his return joined the fledging punk band, X-Ray Spex. After co-writing much of the material for their début album he was sacked from the group for refusing to cut his hair. He later recorded with Essential Logic who were signed to Rough Trade, before returning to Heathrow Airport to work as an export clerk. Wreckage's bassist, John Taylor, became the concert sound engineer with Patto, a band fronted by Mike Patto who released albums firstly with Vertigo and later Island. After Patto folded in the mid-Seventies John drifted into band management and his current clients include the founding member of Traffic, Jim Capaldi, along with Joe and Sam Brown, of the famous Brown musical family which until her premature death also included the singer, Vicky. Mike Bersin worked his way through various jobs in local radio before becoming a director at the Metro Radio Group in Newcastle-upon-Tyne. Mike Smith, meanwhile, was last heard of living in New York in a trailer; he had gone to the United States after marrying an American girl he met in England.

In the autumn of 1969 Freddie moved back to London, disappointed but not disillusioned, now fixated about becoming a pop star. Ibex and Wreckage, in truth, had been average rock groups, content to plagiarise in the main, and only Freddie's input had given them any real panache. It would be easy to consign Freddie's commitment to Ibex/Wreckage as a dalliance, albeit an enthusiastic one. Ken Testi would concur: "I think Ibex filled a gap for Freddie. He wanted to be singing in a band and Ibex benefited enormously from having him. It was a marriage of convenience for all parties. We were all very naïve and there would have been some naïveté in Freddie at that time. To Freddie it was like his first second hand car, the sort of thing you buy when you can just scrape a bit of money together. Eventually you want a better one."

Freddie had cared enormously about Ibex; enough, in fact, to change their name, image, and set (which he was doing towards the end) and temporarily to leave his cherished London. During this period Freddie crackled with ambition and eagerness. His zeal had a profound effect on his newly acquired friends from Liverpool, and for many of them it helped put their own lives, their ambitions and dreams, into perspective. "It was an education knowing Freddie," said Ken. "He was very committed about everything. He had a certain tenacity, a single mindedness, a desire for excellence."

Back in London, Freddie put the word around that he was available for freelance graphic design work, but this was never more than an aside in his mind. Austin Knight's agency in Chancery Lane gave his portfolio tacit approval and promised him some design work, including the drawings for a children's science fiction story. He was also asked to sketch fashion items for a local paper; Mike Bersin remembers looking over his shoulder one day to find him painstakingly drawing a woman wearing a corset! Richard Thompson lent him some aircraft magazines after Freddie was commissioned to illustrate a book about World War I.

He was really set upon stardom at all cost. Making a living from art entailed application beyond his scope, whereas training for the pop business was unspecific. It could be made up as he went along. He was no longer reticent about his desires; he told anyone within earshot that he was going to be a legend, dear boy. He refused to take buses or travel on the tube. He was unknown and almost destitute, but would rather spend money on a taxi fare than a meal. His behaviour seemed a tinge pathetic, deluded even, to some of his friends, and they mused on how Freddie would survive if he did not find his niche. Freddie, the bluster already consummate, would have none of it and for someone who had not written more than the bones of a few songs, his audacity was remarkable.

Around people he already knew, Freddie was very much at ease and often held court with them. Even if he were not talking about anything of real importance, his profuse mannerisms and ardour would make him the pivotal point in a group. He did not have the same air of confidence with strangers; it was often said throughout Queen's career that he was inordinately happy and voluble at his own parties, but quite often a wallflower at those thrown by others.

During the winter of 1969 and spring of 1970 he began to respond to adverts for singers which were placed in the music press. His audition with the group Sour

Milk Sea summed up his personality. He was really extremely nervous of the situation, but conspired to make it appear as if he was self assurance incarnate. He needed moral support and asked Roger Taylor and Smile's roadie, John Harris, to accompany him to their youth club rehearsal room in Dorking. The band had never seen such ostentation. Roger held open the van door for Freddie who stepped out regally, wearing a fur coat, designer trousers and high boots. John Harris followed them into the building, solicitously carrying Freddie's Schure microphone in a wooden box. It was all ridiculously pompous and after such a grand entrance the band were virtually intimidated into giving Freddie the job.

Sour Milk Sea had been formed by Chris Dummett, whose father was a philosophy don at All Souls College, Oxford, and whose mother was a local councillor. The group first came together while its members were pupils at St Edward's School, a minor public school in Oxford. Originally known as Tomato City (which was also the title of one of their songs), the line-up was Chris Dummett on guitar and vocals, Jeremy 'Rubber' Gallop on rhythm guitar, Paul Milne on bass, and Boris Williams on drums. They were each five or six years younger than Freddie and sported the same long hairstyles with brutal centre partings. They had been in existence for nearly a year when Freddie joined and they were keen, rehearsing up to six times each week under their new band name borrowed from the title of a Jackie Lomax song.

Chris Dummett already had a musical history of sorts; he had met Eric Clapton as a teenager, and was eager to sample as much of the scene as possible. He dropped his first acid tab at sixteen and wore his hair long through his later school years. The group had a cosmopolitan attitude to the use of drugs and often rehearsed while stoned or high. They were moulded from a riotous strand of eccentric middle England Bohemia. They once drove from Jeremy Gallop's home town of Leatherhead in Surrey to their rehearsal base in Dorking while on speed and crashed the van into a wall before completing the four-mile journey.

Boris Williams had left the group before Freddie joined. He went in search of the exotic and jumped aboard one of the numerous camper vans voyaging from west London to India. He was to return some years later and join one of new wave's most successful groups, The Cure. His place behind the drum kit in Sour Milk Sea was taken by Rob Tyrell.

Sour Milk Sea, with Chris Dummett taking on vocals by 'default', were heavily influenced by the British blues boom of the Sixties, revering artists like John Mayall, Chicken Shack and the early incarnations of Fleetwood Mac, featuring guitarist Peter Green. They were a band with considerable intent – before most of them had reached seventeen they had supported Deep Purple and P.P. Arnold at venues like the Civic Hall in Guildford. Their experimental bent gave them an edge many others missed. Chris Dummett was happy for his solos to bleed over the music and groups like The Pretty Things, with the inspired live meandering of Twink, had given them a fairly left-field perspective.

They were each interested in developing as virtuoso performers and decided that a singer would free them to indulge themselves as artists. Their equipment was the best available because Jeremy Gallop, whose late father, Clive Gallop, was a wealthy businessman, bought it on their behalf. Jeremy's mother was a cousin of Walter Bentley, one of the famous pioneering 'Bentley Boys'. Their practice room was well stocked with powerful amplifiers and Gibson and Fender guitars.

The response to their advert for a singer in *Melody Maker* was excellent and the applicants were of an unusually high standard. Jeremy Gallop remembers auditioning a black singer with a 'voice sent from God' and Bridget St John, who had recorded an album for John Peel's Dandelion label just a year earlier. She later went on to work with John Martyn and Mike Oldfield among others, but her style hardly fitted with Sour Milk Sea.

Once Freddie walked through the door the decision was a formality. "He was dripping in velvet," said Chris Dummett. "He really turned it on at that first rehearsal. We asked him if he wanted the lyrics to our songs and he said, 'No thanks I've got my own.' He came up to me during one of the guitar solos and was really giving it all the physical gestures. He was a riot of colour, full of confidence, nothing like what we could have ever expected. Afterwards, the band just sat around with this smirk of agreement. We weren't remotely interested in anyone else, he had such enormous charisma."

Freddie told Chris he was a close friend of the members of Smile and Chris gave a knowing snigger. A few months earlier both Sour Milk Sea and Smile had been booked to play at All Saints Hall in Notting Hill Gate, a venue of some magnitude on the hippie/progressive rock scene of the time. Hawkwind, for example, were signed to a record deal on the strength of a ten-minute jam at the hall. A squabble had broken out between Sour Milk Sea and Smile as to who would headline. Chris left his band's manager, Nic Twilley, to resolve the matter while he went to the bar. On his return he learned that Smile would be the main attraction for the night and Nic told him it seemed to matter a great deal to them. "I don't know why it should have particularly," he said. "It was one of those two men and a dog in the audience type of gig."

Sour Milk Sea found bookings easy to come by in Oxford, as it was Chris Dummett's home town. Freddie made his début with them on Friday, March 20, 1970. The band had previously appeared at the city's Randolph Hotel but Freddie's first show was a benefit for Shelter at Highfield Parish Hall, Headington. Also on the bill were The Harlow Go-Gos from nearby Old Marston Secondary School. Bette Jones, the secretary of Shelter's Oxford branch, promised the young punters that the catering would be appropriate - lots of milk and yogurt.

In an unusually contemporary move, the *Oxford Mail* invited Sour Milk Sea to 'have their say' in print as a preview to their appearance. Much of the band's article was drawn from lyrics written by Freddie to a song called 'Lover' which later evolved into 'Liar', a track on Queen's début album. It was a fascinating example of the heartfelt, elegiac, but ultimately vacuous prose which most British bands, famous or not, were dispensing at the time: "You never had it so good. The yoghurt pushers are here. There's a place I have been and a face I have seen today. I have said all my prayers, never answered, never cared at all. But there's a sudden change in me. I'm another person inside of me. Tomorrow I am going to see the last of the blue skies above me. Lover calling, I hear your voice, solar systems that surround you all your life, they remind me that you're really from another source of light. Lover, take me to your leader, I give you body and soul. Come to understand, I grow my life in the palm of your hand."

It was apparent immediately that Freddie and Chris Dummett had a rapport. They both possessed a deep love of music and realised they needed a musical axis in order to focus their songs. "Freddie had a much greater pop sensibility than most people around at that time," said Chris. "We were very blues based while he was into the Move, The Hollies, Steve Winwood, people like that. His was a much broader base of appreciation. I really wanted to learn from him and he was willing to take me under his wing."

The pair formed an extremely close friendship and within weeks Chris had moved in to the house in Ferry Road so they could write songs together. Freddie took it upon himself to inculcate Chris, who was nearly six years younger, with a certain decorum. They shared clothes, listened to records together (especially Hendrix's 'Electric Ladyland' album), and began visiting restaurants. Freddie, eager to embrace the new, patronised a restaurant in Gloucester Terrace, near Paddington station, which specialised in macrobiotic food. "We got on fabulously," said Chris. "He tried to make me aware of my appearance. He was charming and sweet and would share any food he had in the house. He was a very generous and warm person."

Their relationship was platonic, but Chris quickly surmised that Freddie's sexuality was equivocal: "He had someone who he called his girlfriend [this would not appear to have been Mary Austin] but she only came to the house a couple of times. There was no evidence of him ever dipping his wick. He would refer sometimes to his 'bender friends', quite laughingly. He was always very camp and fey, he'd really taken on board all that androgyny package. There was something weird about this 'girlfriend' situation but at seventeen I wasn't equipped to analyse it. He was very proud of having a girlfriend but he wouldn't let you get close to her. He had an attitude that defied you to go further on the subject. It was a case of not showing your lack of social poise by asking further; it would have blown your cool by showing how much you cared. In those days there was an absolute paranoia about staying cool."

Jeremy Gallop was similarly baffled by Freddie's sexuality: "It crossed my mind that he might be queer. He never made eyes at the girls, though he didn't show any signs of being homosexual. I was quite a pretty boy myself in those days but he never came on to me or anything. The rest of us were sniffing out the women but we thought Freddie was cool. We used to think he was so cool he'd get the best looking chicks without even trying."

Chris Dummett fell easily into the erratic lifestyle of 40 Ferry Road and found Freddie an amiable companion. Some nights Freddie would take out his portfolio of drawings; Chris remembers that they each seemed to feature Jimi Hendrix in some way. On some, Jimi was an eighteenth-century dandy, complete with cane, while on others his face was in vivid close-up. While he was living at the house he noticed Roger Taylor had grown a beard. "He did it to stop people saying, 'Can I help you madam?' ," said Chris. "He looked like a fucking girl! Groupies were in and out of the house at all times but no one would fuck them. They were dogs really, put in the spare room. They were desperate girls who nobody fancied. Maybe Tupp Taylor shagged a few of them, he looked like the type who might."

In the household it was generally accepted that Roger, feminine looks or not, was the most successful with girls. On a whim, his friend from Cornwall, Peter Bawden, suggested they should drive out to the Ideal Home Exhibition in Birmingham. "I learned that day that Roger had real magnetism," he said. "It was an education. So many girls were making plays for him it was unbelievable. We'd gone there just for a lark but all eyes were watching this good looking blond guy. He didn't even have to chat them up, his strike-rate was unbelievable."

The addition of Freddie to Sour Milk Sea brought almost a complete transition to their music and shifted the balance of control. Freddie insisted on singing his own words to songs they had already written, and while Chris Dummett admired this fresh, single-minded approach, the others, especially Paul Milne, largely saw it as usurpation. The new songs drafted in by Freddie and Chris were 'architectural in concept' - they carried unexpected changes of tempo and unusual stage dynamics. At their handful of concerts, however, the band were unanimous about Freddie's ability "He just seemed to turn on a light," said Chris Dummett. "He used to plan things beforehand and had this great patter with the audience. He was cynical but witty with it. At the end of a song he sometimes said very quickly into the microphone, 'Wank you,' and you could see the audience thinking, "Did he say 'Thank you', or 'Wank You' just then?"

Relations in Sour Milk Sea were strained when it became obvious that Freddie, with Chris Dummett's support, was out to change their sound. "Quite early on he started to change it," said Jeremy Gallop. "It was awkward at the time and caused a few rifts. The thing I remember most about Freddie was that he was a wonderful arbitrator. I was pretty fiery but he was a very good calming influence. He was a good speaker and had this gentle way with him." There was a disagreement about introducing Freddie's song 'Lover' into their set. "I just didn't like it, and Chris did," says Gallop. "It was dynamic pop and a little bit twee. He was trying to bring a commercial edge to the band and we saw ourselves as an underground band, quite cerebral I suppose. When you're a kid, and we all were at the time, all this sort of thing matters a great deal. Freddie was really the wrong choice for Sour Milk Sea but I felt he was manipulating Chris. Chris was head over heels in love with Freddie so to speak. We were supposed to be a heavy duty blues band but Freddie was coming up with these huge harmonies even then. His ideas seemed really difficult to do and I thought we were going to end up sounding like The Dolly Sisters if we started singing all those harmonies. Eventually we started thinking, 'Fuck Fred, we'll do it our way'."

A rift developed thereafter between Chris Dummett and Freddie and the other members of Sour Milk Sea and by the spring of 1970 the band was set to disintegrate. It was inevitable that Jeremy Gallop would feel most upset because he and Chris Dummett had originally formed the group and Jeremy was about to lose his much-valued musical partner. As well as time and effort, Jeremy had invested a great deal of money in the band. At the age of nineteen he spent £8,000 of inheritance money on a motorcycle and equipment for the band. He had bought the best Ampeg amplifiers imported from the United States, a new transit van, and kitted everyone out with the best available instruments. The money aside, Sour Milk Sea was, as is often the case with teenage dreams, 'his world'.

Jeremy Gallop was angered more by Chris Dummett than Freddie. He recognised that Freddie was, to a degree, orchestrating the split, tempting Chris away for his own designs. Yet he saw Chris's ready compliance as nothing short of betrayal. The pair, although close friends even now, always had a tempestuous rapport. On one occasion Jeremy had thrown a cup of hot coffee over Chris during a band argument and fled to the toilets, locking himself in before Chris could gain retribution. "There were a few nasty moments when all this was going down," said Jeremy. "Freddie didn't care that he was splitting up the group. You have got to be ruthless to get anywhere. Everyone is selfish to a point when you're trying to make it. There was tension for a while but I never had any argument with Freddie, in fact I liked him a great deal. The thing was I'd put my life into the group and it was hideous that it should end. I was in tears over it, it was like the end of the world. I was sad about losing Chris, I wasn't bothered about losing Freddie at all. Freddie was obviously a pop singer and I wasn't into that at all, but Chris was an amazing lead guitarist, a real hot shot, and I thought my chances of making it were a lot slimmer without having him around."

Quite rightly, Jeremy Gallop felt that once Sour Milk Sea had split Chris Dummett should return the Gibson SG guitar and Marshall stack he had bought for him. He considered it an implicit agreement that the equipment was provided on condition it was used in Sour Milk Sea. "It was very unpleasant getting the stuff back from Chris," Gallop recalls. "I was nervous about driving round to Ferry Road to pick it up. I was scared of getting my head kicked in. I knew if Freddie was in there would be no trouble because he was so diplomatic. Luckily he was, and I got it back, though it was made obvious to me that Chris was really pissed off."

The retrieval of the equipment scuppered the short-term plans of Chris and Freddie. "I was planning to form another band with Freddie but not having a guitar and not having much money put a kibosh on the idea," said Chris.

Chris Dummett was given an early insight into the relationship between Freddie and his future musical collaborators, Brian May and Roger Taylor. He could sense a bizarre 'courtship' between them which would remain unconsummated for some time yet. "Brian May was light years ahead of me but he did not have any fire in his bollocks," Dummett claims. "Freddie thought Brian was suburban and droopy. I think, for their part, the Smile people thought of Freddie as a little bit of a joke. They used to send him up, take the piss a bit, in an affectionate way I suppose."

He detected that Freddie was aspiring to replace Tim Staffell and was quite focused on doing so, though he doubts whether he would have engineered anything particularly devious. "Freddie had to eliminate Tim because he had such a strong voice," Dummett points out. "Freddie could be very strong-willed, single-minded. Tim did not have the pizazz like Freddie. Tim, at the time, was much more rounded in terms of musicianship but Freddie was the definite extrovert." Tim Staffell did not suspect Freddie of any covert chicanery. He was, in fact, pleased to leave Smile and move in a new musical direction and was quite apathetic about who took over his position in Smile, or any group formed from their ashes.

For a number of years Freddie Mercury, Brian May and Roger Taylor had formed a close social grouping. They had lived, worked and played together. It had not been a dry, cordial arrangement; there had been rows and fights, pettiness and gravity, and it was perhaps too obvious, too mawkish even, that this family of three should form itself into a pop group. Once Tim Staffell had moved on and Sour Milk Sea had floundered, however, it was impossible for them to avoid the inevitable and when Brian May returned from Tenerife in April 1970, he, Roger and Freddie finally decided to form their first group together. They planned it in meticulous detail; they had all been part of strong, but ultimately unfulfilled groups in the recent past and were now resolute about the success of any new venture together.

They discussed several potential band names. An early favourite was The Grand Dance, drawn from C.S. Lewis' books, *Out Of The Silent Planet*, a trilogy both Brian and Roger had read. The Rich Kids (later adopted by Glen Matlock's post-Pistols outfit) was another candidate, but Freddie, with his usual imperiousness, had settled defiantly on Queen. "It's ever so regal," he claimed to anyone in earshot. Roger Taylor's mother, Win Hitchens remembers Freddie's spirited explanation in the kitchen of her Truro home: "He just kept saying how regal it sounded," she said.

Like everyone else, Win Hitchens also recognised its flagrant nod to homosexuality, most pointedly the greasepaint, theatrical strand to which Freddie aspired. In the early Seventies the word 'gay' was rarely used to describe homosexuality. 'Queen', though now largely archaic, was a more usual colloquialism. Several of Freddie's friends called him affectionately 'the old queen' and this reversal of gender terminology was often used in an ironic way. Elton John, who became a close friend and confidante, invariably said 'she' or 'her' when talking of Freddie. 'Queen', however, was not merely a nickname of Freddie's;

in appearance at least it could equally have applied to both Roger and Brian. At this time Brian was wearing flared jeans with tiny bells sewn around the bottom of each leg. His hair was past his shoulders and necklaces dangled loosely around his neck. Roger and Brian were unconvinced of its qualities as a band name, but Freddie was persuasive and by the end of April 1970 they were Queen.

Enter, Stage Right

Chapter VIII

Queen

The word 'hype' is passé and rarely used these days in music business circles. There are substitute words, still hyperbolic, which drape shadows more elegantly across the shabby dealings which see one artist placed before another in terms of promotion and profile. This can take many forms: record shop window displays, column inches and adverts in the music press, giant posters plastered on disused warehouses on the outskirts of town or, at its most venal, assisted passage up the charts through the discreet distribution of envelopes containing cash or drugs.

At any one time a major record label may have a roster of more than 50 acts, but only a handful will receive a substantial promotional budget. Of this handful most will be established acts, so the label spends a great deal to recoup a great deal. New acts are promoted in various ways – some are given a reasonable budget and left to smoulder, others are set alight immediately and burnt into your consciousness, but often labels are indiscriminate; in the parlance of the business, they fire the shit against the wall and if it sticks the big promotional push inevitably follows.

When Queen were thrust on to the scene by EMI Records in 1973, the word hype was still in vogue and many felt it applied to the band. The term was not used in its real sense of actual cheating, more as a euphemism for money wasted on something frivolous, on a group who did not warrant or deserve such financial speculation. It was, in Queen's case, a cruel, baseless slur. The four years between their formation and first hit, 1970 to 1974, were onerous. It was largely a succession of rebuffs and disappointments and it was during these often dark days that the self-belief, vision, impudence and guarded personality of Queen was formed.

The ill-fortune began almost immediately. After Freddie Mercury, Roger Taylor and Brian May became Queen, it would take them nearly a year even to complete the line-up, an inordinately long time to find a suitable bass player. Mike Grose, a Cornish friend of Roger Taylor, had sometimes filled in for Tim Staffell when Smile played shows in the West Country, so he was an obvious candidate to replace him permanently. Mike was busy in Truro, managing PJs and playing in various bands, but he responded to Roger's invitation and moved to London to join Queen.

They practised once or twice each week at Imperial College and often held impromptu rehearsals in the garden at Ferry Road. There, songs later known for their robust, amplified power like 'Keep Yourself Alive' and 'Seven Seas Of Rhye' were schemed on acoustic guitars. Mike Grose remembers the constant, but good-natured bickering of Roger and Freddie, and the quiet assurance of Brian.

Queen's first live appearance under their new name was at the City Hall, Truro, on Saturday June 27, 1970. The concert had been arranged some time earlier, when they were still known as Smile, and in the local Cornish papers they were billed under their former name. The concert was partly arranged by Roger Taylor's mother, Win Hitchens, to raise money for the Red Cross. Queen received £50 expenses and the price of admission for the show which also boasted a guest DJ, Jeff Spence, was 7s/6d. They opened their set with 'Stone Cold Crazy', a track loosely based on a Wreckage number. The concert hall was only half-full, and though the band looked striking in their monochrome silk costumes, even Win Hitchens considered them more than a shade unpolished. "Freddie was not like how he became," she said. "He had not got his movements off properly."

It was perhaps appropriate that the first show to be billed properly under their new name should be at their natural home, Imperial College, in London's SW7. Freddie designed hand-drawn tickets which bore a scratchy but florid outline of the word 'Queen' in a similar typeface to that which would later adorn their record sleeves. The ticket, which also included a map showing the college's proximity to South Kensington tube station, read: 'Queen invite you to a private showing at Imperial College New Block, Imperial Institute Road, Level 5, Lecture Theatre A on Sunday 18 July'.

The band, on only their second show together and with a bassist still settling in, had been impetuous in holding such an early 'showcase'. Ultimately, it hardly mattered since interest in them from the music business was negligible. They were still a homespun affair, there had been no covert business strategy behind their formation, much of it was carried out on impulse and enthusiasm. They were, to their credit, extremely enthusiastic, much of this being down to Freddie. They openly solicited their friends' comments about performances and were not afraid of criticism. They asked "What did you think?" until the entreaty became almost tiresome.

Their set was composed almost entirely of cover versions and for some time they included just two of their own songs, 'Stone Cold Crazy' and 'Liar'. They would open the set with the former, one of the few songs to develop from a group jamming session and to feature the whole group as co-writers. Their repertoire of covers was rich and, depending on audience reaction, they would plunder material by Buddy Holly, James Brown, The Everly Brothers, Gene Vincent, Little Richard, Ricky Nelson, Shirley Bassey, Bill Haley, The Spencer Davis Group and The Yardbirds. Queen had no strategy to challenge their audience and there was no esoteric agenda, unlike many of their peers. "We did more heavy rock'n'roll with the Queen delivery to give people something they could get hold of – get on, sock it to 'em, get off," said Brian May. "If you go on stage and people don't know your material, you can get boring." Clearly, Queen as the compliant, pop-orientated force was fashioned from the beginning.

Queen returned to Cornwall on July 25 to appear at PJ's in Truro and afterwards Mike Grose informed them that he intended to stay in Cornwall and quit the band after just three concerts with them. "I left Queen because I'd had enough of playing basically," he said. "I had just got to that point. We weren't earning any money to speak of, and we were living in squalor. I just didn't want to be part of it any more. Brian had another year of his studies to go, and so did Roger – and I thought to hell with it." Mike had a feeling 'in his bones' that Queen would make it, but after a long, long slog of seven years in his home county with various unfulfilled groups he had reached a point where his greatest opportunity had come too late. Unlike Brain and Roger, who were also partly focused on college studies (though Roger was taking a year out between leaving the dentistry course and beginning another in biology at North London Polytechnic), Queen would have been his complete immediate future, and he had no 'safety net' of possible alternative employment.

Mike Grose stayed in Cornwall and established his own haulage business in St Austell. He is still tracked down intermittently by journalists hoping to find the 'Pete Best' or 'Stuart Sutcliffe' of Queen, but he is weary of the chase and now turns down all requests for interviews. "I've said what I've got to say already, it's in all the other books," is the stock response.

Queen found a replacement bassist when two Rogers met in Cornwall – Roger Taylor and Roger Crossley. A Londoner on holiday in Cornwall, Roger Crossley told Roger Taylor about his friend living in north London, Barry Mitchell, a bass player without a band. On his return to the capital Roger contacted Mitchell and after just one rehearsal at Imperial College he was made a member of Queen in the summer of 1970. He joined the group just a few weeks before the death of Jimi Hendrix on September 18. Freddie and Roger closed their market stall that day as a mark of respect to their musical hero and Freddie travelled over to an art gallery in Launceston Place, Kensington, where Chris Dummett was working. "Freddie came in and said Jimi had died," said Chris Dummett. "He was devastated and so was I. He wasn't crying, Freddie was always pretty much battened down, he had everything under control. I remember I asked for the day off work but the boss wouldn't let me."

Barry Mitchell's musical progression had been uncannily similar to that of Brian May and Roger Taylor, although it had perhaps taken in more of the industry's shenanigans. He started at Clearmont School, Harrow, playing Shadows' covers in a group known as The Nameless Ones. They evolved into Conviction, a soul covers band, with a guitarist who later became very famous – Alan Parsons. Conviction discovered rock and took on the name Earth, just a few weeks before the band which later became Black Sabbath adopted the same name. The Birmingham group quickly rescinded and the London-based Earth landed themselves a residency at The Coffin Club, housed in the former premises of Ronnie Scott's in Gerrard Street, London. Their sets were sometimes six hours long and would involve guest spots where whimsical acts like Whistling Concrete, nothing more than a hippy playing the flute, would share the stage.

They acquired a fast-talking manager, Douglas Mew, and he tried to persuade them to change their name to London. They later discovered he had previously worked with a disbanded group called London and was still hopeful of utilising their promotional material. Mew paid for them to record an album – ten songs in one day, no less – but the record did not materialise beyond acetate stage.

The album, had it been released, would have caused quite a stir. Relying heavily on Mitchell's elaborate but fluid bass style, it was a rich meander through a swampy blues tenor, especially on songs like 'Rain On The Roof' and the anguished tail-out track, 'Angel Of Death'.

Barry Mitchell left Earth to adopt the posture and raucous bliss of The Jimi Hendrix Experience in a group called Black. Fronted by Pete Lewis, a black South African with a strong resemblance to Hendrix, they had a moderate degree of success. They were managed by Gerry Horgan, an early ally of Cat Stevens, and he secured them a deal with the music publishers, Francis, Day and Hunter, a company which later had a tenuous business link with Queen.

When Black folded, Mitchell had become ambivalent about a career in music but still agreed to audition with Queen. "The band struck me as being heavily into Led Zeppelin and Hendrix and in some respects they sounded a lot like Zeppelin," he said. "I was in straight away, after the first rehearsal. They just checked me out to see whether I could play or not." It was surprising that Mitchell's initiation was so guileless; there had been no element of 'sounding him out' – he could play, so he was in, without any real consideration of his appearance (which was certainly more unrefined than theirs) or his personality, musical or otherwise. If they had asked, they would have discovered he was fatigued with rock and intent on playing jazz or in bands with a brass section.

Barry Mitchell's first show with Queen was at Imperial College on August 23 and it gave him an early taste of their idiosyncrasies. Fundamentally a seasoned rocker, he found himself beforehand in the kitchen of Brian May's flat making popcorn to give out to the crowd. Freddie, who made little attempt to get to know Mitchell, spent several weeks telling everyone he intended to take the stage wearing a dress. The 'dress' was in fact a one-piece body suit, open to the waist to reveal his chest. Freddie dubbed it his 'Mercury' suit and had one in black and another in white.

Although his tenure in Queen was brief – just eleven shows in a six month period - Barry Mitchell had long enough to assess their individual personalities: "Brian was the most instantly likeable. He was very approachable. Roger was a typical drummer, a ladies' man and good fun. Freddie looked very different and called everyone 'darling' or 'sweetie'. He used to use heated curlers in his hair and it wasn't what I was used to at all. He looked more foreign in those days, his skin seemed darker and his teeth were more prominent. In fact, they were extremely prominent, I'm sure he had them done later on. When I was in the band his hand was always up to his mouth as if he was trying to hide them."

Mitchell shared the opinion of Queen held by most people within the music business at the time - that they weren't particularly original. "I didn't think they were going anywhere," he said. "It never struck me as being great, it never felt like that for me. They were striving for something that was already there - Led Zeppelin, but I didn't want to go there, I wanted to do something different."

There is no question that Queen had a strong fixation with Led Zeppelin at this time. Several friends recall Freddie's enthusiasm for the group vividly. If a Led Zeppelin track was played on the radio or on someone's tape recorder at Kensington Market, he would demand silence and later deconstruct the song, usually enthusing about its extraordinary power. Surprisingly, Freddie seemed most interested in the wall of guitar built by Jimmy Page. Richard Thompson saw the band at The Marquee with Freddie, and afterwards he hardly mentioned Robert Plant, it was the overall sound of Led Zeppelin that fascinated him. Freddie often said he wanted to infuse the same sense of space and dynamism into Queen's music.

Freddie was flamboyant at rehearsals, but Barry Mitchell didn't feel the posture was matched by the voice: "He didn't sing very well, that was self evident. It just wasn't there, it would break up and he couldn't hold the note. It was later on, in the Eighties, when it really became spot-on. Brian was outstanding, technically brilliant. Roger was never a great drummer but I loved his backing vocal harmonies, his high-pitched stuff."

In rehearsal Freddie did not play either guitar or piano and, indeed, Mitchell was unaware he could play an instrument. Despite this, Freddie appeared to form the group's musical core. "It was Freddie who had the ideas, most of them came from him," he said. "If someone else came up with something Freddie would hone it until it was right. Freddie had this really clear vision of how the songs should go."

One of the more common voices of dissent belonged to the band's roadie, John Harris – famous for his leather trousers – whose selfless commitment to the group surprised Barry Mitchell. "John was always at rehearsals," he said. "He would help them pull all the gear out and he really cared about them. There was no mixing desk for him to use, so there wasn't a lot he could do about the actual sound. He would be the mediator if Freddie was in one of his moodies. The band respected him and he sometimes tried to bully them into playing well, but it wasn't easy because they were strong guys. There were no real arguments, just the usual stuff about how long the solos should go on for, that kind of thing."

Mitchell contributed little in the way of songwriting. At the time the band were forming the material which would appear on their début album released nearly three years later. He did not consider himself a writer and usually adapted bass lines already mapped out by either Tim Staffell, Mike Grose, or Brian May. He was unsure of how his rather busy playing style went down with the other members, and they rarely made any comments candidly to him. He noted afterwards that John Deacon's direct technique was the antithesis of his own.

Barry Mitchell decided to leave Queen at the end of 1970 and his final shows with them were on January 8 and 9, 1971, at The Marquee and Ewell Technical College, Surrey, when Queen were part of a support bill to Kevin Ayres And The Whole World which also included Genesis. During his last few weeks with Queen there had been a perceptible change in their outlook. "Their ambition had started to develop," Mitchell explains. "It had a different feel somehow. I started to realise that they were taking it seriously and wanted to go places. I still didn't think they would make it because they weren't truly original or obviously commercial. I just didn't like their music, and I didn't rate it through most of the Seventies, all that 'Night At The Opera' and fairy stuff. I felt that way until I saw them at Live Aid when I thought they were astonishing."

Mary Austin, with whom Freddie was now living in Holland Park, made a vague plea for Barry Mitchell to remain with the band, but the others accepted his decision unequivocally. Barry Mitchell had brass sections and something a little more direct or original in mind, and soon afterwards found himself in Crushed Butler, a band which he felt predated The Jam by a number of years. They earned a few one-line mentions in *NME* and once supported Atomic Rooster at Guildford Civic Hall, but it was small change compared to the success of his former group. "I've never regretted the decision because the group I left was nothing like the one it later became," he said. "At the time I made the decision which was right for me. I just wasn't happy playing their music and wanted to do other things."

He lost touch with Queen afterwards but was happy to see Roger Taylor, with whom he had started to establish a friendship, soon after the release of Queen's first album. "A friend of mine had seen Roger at the Marquee and he told Roger that I was working at Lasky's in Oxford Street," he said. "Roger came round and checked me out. I think he wanted to buy a hi-fi at the time." Their next meeting was two decades later when Barry Mitchell, his long blond hair now a thinning recollection, went backstage after Roger's solo performance at the Cambridge Junction in 1994: "It was hard for him to recognise me, he had a puzzled look on his face. He finally remembered and said, 'It's been a fucking long time!'. He remembered that I lived at Kingsbury, which I was surprised about because it's only a small place."

Queen's third bassist in just seven months was 'Doug'; few people around the band bothered to inquire his surname, though 'Ewood' has fastened itself to some hazy memories. Again, it was another heedless choice and Doug appeared with the band on only two occasions – at Hornsey Town Hall on February 19, 1971, and Kingston Polytechnic the following day. These were two prestigious shows, both in support of Yes, and Doug's stage manner rather spoiled the occasion, at least as far as the other members of Queen were concerned. Clearly the unspoken communiqué was that Freddie held centre stage, the rest were to play vital and colourful supporting roles, but make no attempt to steal the show. Doug broke this accord in startling manner, jumping up and down and choreographing his own personal stage routine. In Queen's semi-official ('Written in co-operation with...') biography, Brian May referred to Doug's stage manner scornfully as 'most incongruous'. The situation was addressed immediately and categorically - Doug was fired on February 21, the day after the Kingston gig, and three days in the life of Queen would seem to summarise this musical comet called Doug.

Queen were hardly judicious in their choice of bassists, so it was merely the law of averages that finally brought a turn in fortune. John Deacon was a lucky accident for Queen; they had already gone through three bassists but to find someone so complementary to their sound, professionalism and personalities could well have taken for ever.

John Deacon had revealed very little of himself to most people on the Leicester scene. He was far from charismatic, he was the quiet one, and, they naturally assumed, the insignificant one. He would go to London, earn a degree, marry another scholar, return to Leicester, and set up a small electronics company. The members of his former group, The Opposition, Nigel Bullen especially, knew John beyond this superficiality. They respected his quiet determination, the innate integrity, a meticulousness of character. They knew he wouldn't be on the first train home. He wasn't a minor key dreamer; he had more blood in him than many suspected.

Initially, they presumed he would apply himself solely to his studies; he left his guitars and amplifier behind in Oadby. Whatever, they knew he would survive in London. The city might have lost its technicolour glow somewhat since 1966 but it was still fast, radiant, wide and simmering to a kid from the hush of rural middle England. He didn't re-invent himself at university, but like millions before and since, found himself; to such an extent that by the end of his university course he all but severed completely his ties with his former self in Oadby.

During the first couple of years at university he returned quite regularly to Leicester, sometimes even sitting in with Art or other groups featuring his old pals from The Opposition. Of his small circle of friends only Dave Williams and Nigel Bullen kept in close contact, Nigel sometimes staying with John for the weekend at the top floor flat he shared with four other male students in Queensgate. There was still no dabbling in drugs and only a mild dalliance in alcohol. Instead, Deacon absorbed himself in London's burgeoning counter-culture - clothes from Sterling Cooper and Kensington Market, exhibitions by Roger Ruskin Spear of The Bonzo Dog Doo-Dah Band in The Strand. "He was really enjoying it," said Nigel. "There was a definite change. He became very trendy, grew his hair long. He was the same academically, he still sat down and did his work, but he came out of himself socially which was good. He was holding his own among it very well."

Distance harboured nostalgia. John Deacon had left Oadby to embrace academia and London and he felt he no longer had any need for his guitar or amplifier. By turns, he succumbed once more to the lure of the plectrum. On one trip home he collected his acoustic guitar and soon afterwards asked his mother to drive down with his bass and amplifier. Suddenly, less than a year after leaving The Opposition, he wanted to be part of a group again.

This was London though, completely different from Leicester. Its live circuit was glamour itself; a venue in Leicester was a church hall or the back room of a pub, in London it was The Marquee and Jimi Hendrix had been there just a few years earlier, and David Bowie. The entire history of rock, it seemed, was condensed in a handful of venues, and administered within a few square miles of the capital. Music writers, managers, and record company staff perused these darkened venues, like extras from Expresso Bongo, except now they wore stack-heeled boots and baggy denims: 'We'll make you famous, man. Here's my card.' In the morning, sometime around 11.30 am, they were in their Soho offices, gold records on the wall, sunglasses on, two aspirins in the glass, trying to fathom the office tape machine. It was less than 100 miles from Leicester, but still a world away.

John Deacon's return to music was tentative at first, galvanised by attending concerts at the colleges around the Kensington area. In October, 1970, he saw a group bathed in shadows playing peculiar, but unremarkable rock at Kensington's College of Estate Management. They were called Queen, but he could barely distinguish them from the multitude of similar bands swayed by the darkened melodrama of Led Zeppelin.

He began practising with flatmate and guitarist Peter Stoddart, and they were soon joined in their vague blues jams by fellow students, drummer Don Cater and a guitarist known to them only as Albert. They made just one appearance, at Chelsea College in November 1970, playing blues covers and chart hits in support of two other groups. As they needed a name to put on posters, the quartet became 'Deacon' for the night, presumably decided at short notice because of its simplicity, rather than as an appeasement to a newly discovered ego.

At this point John Deacon was an accomplished bassist with top notch equipment. He enjoyed jamming with his friends, but wanted something more.

Back in Oadby he had been through the process of forming and running his own group and had developed as a musician. He was now confident enough of his ability, and carried with him the degree of experience to audition for established groups. He began responding to adverts in *Melody Maker* and was not afraid to aim comparatively high, sitting in with several signed bands. He wasn't offered any positions, but wrote home to his old friend Nigel Bullen in Oadby and said he wasn't too perturbed because it was all valuable experience.

In the midst of such formal approaches, John Deacon found himself a group by chance. Early in 1971 he went along to a disco at the Maria Assumpta Teacher Training College with his friend Peter Stoddart and Peter's friend, Christine Farnell. John was introduced to two friends of Christine's, Roger Taylor and Brian May. They explained that they were in a group called Queen but had just lost their bass player.

They met again a few days later in a lecture room at Imperial College which they were using as a rehearsal base. John had brought along a small practice amp which the others teased him about. They ran through a few original numbers which John was told to feel his way through, and Brian taught him the chords to 'Son And Daughter', a song which became the B-side of Queen's first ever single. They finished with the obligatory blues jam, and before the end the original three members of Queen were confident they had found their final member. "We thought he was great," said Roger Taylor. "We were all so used to each other, and were so over the top. We thought that because he was quiet he would fit in with us without too much upheaval. He was a great bass player too – and the fact that he was a wizard with electronics was definitely a deciding factor."

John Deacon was not the only musician to audition with Queen at Imperial College that day. Also invited was Chris Dummett, Freddie's cohort from Sour Milk Sea. Although a great fan of Brian May's technical ability, Freddie possibly felt the sound needed 'thickening' and that the group could accommodate two guitarists. "Getting me in there was just a bee in Freddie's mind," said Chris Dummett. "Me and Freddie got on well, there was a physical empathy. Brian was kind of limp and Freddie missed getting a reaction. Freddie liked and enjoyed a foil and I was happy to play ball. Freddie asked me to join Queen and thought it would work."

Chris Dummett did not have equipment and had to borrow Brian May's at the audition. He was passed the Red Special and it proved to be his downfall. The guitar, with its highly sensitive fret board, required an idiosyncratic playing style. Chris Dummett's fingers 'slid all over it' and few of the notes he played were in time or tune; he didn't even bother to ask whether he'd got the gig or not.

Apart from John Harris, Chris Dummett was the only outsider present at this first ever airing of Queen's finalised line-up. As soon as John Deacon had left the room, his opinion was sought by Brian May. "As well as auditioning myself, they'd asked me down to pass judgement on their new bass player," he said. "John Deacon played with mega efficiency, and zero imagination. He plugged a gap and didn't drop a fucking beat, he was that tight." Incidentally, Chris Dummett had seen Queen perform with Barry Mitchell at Imperial College and had recognised immediately that he was in the wrong band. "He had blond hair and looked like a brickie," he said. "He was obviously a misfit, very different from the others."

Chris Dummett drifted out of the lives of Freddie Mercury and Queen when he returned to his home town to study at Oxford University's New College. He later returned to the guitar, playing in the United States with Mandrake before returning to London where he was a prime mover on the prospering punk scene. Malcolm McLaren invited him to give guitar lessons to the nascent Sex Pistols and he was a member of an early incarnation of Chelsea with Gene October, Tony James and Billy Idol. He also toured as a member of Ben E King's backing group, under the name Chris Chesney; Chesney being his middle name.

He remained in the pop business working behind the scenes on promotional videos and early in 1987 he was alongside David Mallett filming the video for Freddie Mercury's solo single, 'The Great Pretender'. He was apprehensive about meeting Freddie again, intimidated by the disparity of their lives. He tried to blend in with the scenery at A and R Studios in London's Brent Cross but Freddie spotted him and immediately adjourned the shoot. "He took me into this room and said, 'What do you want to drink?'" Dummett recalls. "He put down a line of coke and insisted I took it. He then asked for chilled vodka and we had lots of drink and coke simultaneously. He launched into a rap as though I had seen him yesterday. He was telling me all about his solo records."

When they emerged from the room they walked together to the dressing room where a handful of people were sitting around discussing the video. Chris Dummett noticed the immediate change in Freddie's demeanour: "It was Freddie the performer. He was coming out with all these gags and quips, playing to the gallery. As soon as he entered the room where there were other people it was like a curtain going up. There was definitely two different people in Freddie, two entities. It was part of his armoury as a performer, he could just throw a switch. And yet, one to one, Freddie was as warm a person as you could meet. There was no hidden agenda with him. He was just dedicated to music." The old friends parted company with Freddie announcing to anyone in earshot, "I might get Chris to play on my album." He didn't play on the record, and it was to be their last reunion.

Council Of War

Chapter IX

Queen

Until John Deacon walked into their rehearsal room, the genesis of Queen had been an erratic, hesitant affair. Numerous lives had intertwined but few had run in parallel for any real length of time. Unknown to any of them, they had finally found a line-up which would last them more than 20 years, and one that only death would fracture.

The finalised Queen failed to inspire anything more than the customary apathy from the music business. They had trouble finding concerts even in the capital with its surfeit of venues, and had to call on old friends like Ken Testi. The former 'manager' of Ibex had returned to St Helen's to retake his 'A' levels in the autumn of 1970 and had established himself as social secretary at the local technical college. Although the concerts at St Helen's College were held in a gymnasium, Ken Testi, with his usual wily enthusiasm, had brought artists like Dave Edmunds and Delroy Williams to Merseyside.

He received a phone call from Freddie Mercury informing him that he, Roger and Brian had formed Queen. Instinctively he knew their new group would be 'absolutely wonderful'. "It couldn't be anything else because it contained so much talent," said Testi. "I suppose it hadn't made sense that Freddie wasn't in Smile. He was very much part of their group of friends. Smile had three front-line vocalists and while I think it was mentioned earlier that Freddie should join, Freddie must have been satisfied that they didn't need a singer."

Queen's first concert in Merseyside was at the college on October 30, 1970, while Barry Mitchell was still part of the line up on bass. Partly to make the trip north worthwhile, they appeared at The Cavern Club in Liverpool the following night. The Cavern, made famous, of course, by The Beatles, was six years past its best and known within Liverpool as 'a bit of a toilet', but Queen were delighted to appear there. They spent the night with Ken Testi's family who were running the Market Hotel in St Helen's town centre.

It was the first time Ken Testi had heard or seen the band perform and he admired their resolve: "This was a college in the industrial north and they were this act from Kensington who had come with their posturing and their little grandiose remarks, playing in a gymnasium and getting away with it. They left no one with any doubt they meant it and it was a joy to see." Ken had been a shade concerned about Freddie's routine with the top half of the microphone stand: "I took him to task about that and he said, 'It's my gimmick, my dear. You have got to have a gimmick.' When Freddie expressed conviction like that, argument was pointless." Queen returned again to Merseyside just a few days before the Christmas of 1970 when they played once more at the college and at St Helen's Congregational Church Hall. Their set was still mainly composed of covers but they had devised their own mini-epic, 'Hangman', a track they played live until 1975 but never included on an official record release.

Queen were determined to present a show of consummate professionalism and spent much of the early part of 1971 locked away in rehearsal. They were working on material to be included later on their first two albums and their sedulous approach meant honing the songs took many weeks. They had a fresh confidence in the new line-up but both Brian May and John Deacon were heavily constrained by their college studies. They still managed to rehearse up to four times each week but concerts a good distance from London were virtually impossible during term time. This cautious strategy was to last some time, Brian May not dedicating himself solely to the band until 'Queen II' and John Deacon until 'Sheer Heart Attack'. Whether driven by the need to appease their parents or not, it revealed an astounding degree of prudence – it indubitably slowed Queen's progress in their formative years but these very attributes were later part of their character; they didn't take risks, the group was scrupulously regimented. It was perhaps simultaneously their main strength and weakness.

John Deacon made his live début at Surrey College on July 2, 1971, and the evening was marked by a disagreement between him and Freddie Mercury. Like the group's previous bassists he was primarily a jeans and T-shirt man, but Freddie had singled out a particular shirt he wanted him to wear. John Deacon acquiesced and over the course of the next few years his style of dress was to change markedly.

After a show at Imperial College on July 11, when they again distributed popcorn to the audience, Queen embarked on an 11-date tour of Cornwall, organised by Roger Taylor. It was an excuse to spend more than a month drifting through some of England's finest scenery and they mixed well with Roger's old friends. There were few quarrels and the intensive nature of the trip was an excellent rehearsal for a real life on the road that would follow some time later. They opened at The Garden in Penzance and continued to take their profuse rock to the most unlikely places. Hayle Rugby Club (twice), the NCO's Mess in Culdrose, Truro, and Wadebridge Young Farmers' Club all welcomed Queen, and it was in these inauspicious venues that they learned to temper their lavish pretensions with a common touch which later endeared them to millions.

The apex of their short tour was an appearance at the grandiosely titled Tregaye Festival of Contemporary Music at Tregaye Country Club in Carnon Downs, Truro. The festival on August 21 was partly organised by Roger Taylor's friend, Rik Evans, who supplied the canvas to cover most of the walled garden where the groups played. The line-up was indeed contemporary, with Arthur Brown's Kingdom Come headlining above Hawkwind, The Duster Bennett Band, Tea And Symphony, Brewer's Droop, Indian Summer and Graphite. Queen were second from bottom of the bill, with only Barracuda beneath them. The posters featured a naked girl playing a flute in the mandatory floppy hat, and revellers were promised, 'Food, freaks, licensed bar, and lovely things' for their £1.25 entrance fee.

Ken Testi remained in St Helen's to study, with intermittent forays into London primarily to help Queen. None of them had any real knowledge of the intricacies of the music business and much of their action (or non-action) was decided on impulse. Queen's 'office' became a public telephone at the end of an aisle on Kensington Market and their plan of attack on the industry amounted to Ken Testi procuring a copy of Yellow Pages and working his way through the listed record companies. "We had all this great music on tape and would sit around saying, 'This is great, we should get a record deal'," Testi explained. "But we didn't know how to make the next step. None of us knew much about it and it did become frustrating. I used to ring up record companies and tell them I had this great demo by a wonderful band. We were all young and stupid in those days."

Ken Testi would ring record companies twice, firstly to discover the name of a member of the A&R team, and then to ask for that person by name a few hours later. Amazingly, two companies, EMI and Decca, agreed to meet Ken and the band to listen to their music. All the group attended these meetings, except

John Deacon, who was preoccupied with his studies. Ken Testi remembers Roger Taylor being the most enthusiastic: "He was always ready to drop a lecture for virtually anything." Both EMI and Decca paid mere lip service to Queen and the meetings were fruitless.

Very quickly Ken Testi learned that, as in any business, most of it was done on recommendation. The record industry was inherently unsettled by the new; demo tapes sent without a prior call or nod from an insider were deemed 'idiot tapes' and left to pile up in the corner until the cleaner was finally given permission to scoop up the mound of rotting dreams and put them in the bin.

Due to an unusual dash of good fortune, Queen were at least able to present record companies with a noteworthy demo tape. After returning from Cornwall, Brian May met up with an acquaintance called Terry Yeadon. Originally from Blackburn, Yeadon had moved to London in the mid-Sixties to work as a maintenance engineer at Pye Recording Studios at Marble Arch. He had first met Brian May in 1969 when he attended a Smile concert at Imperial College and afterwards spoke with the group. Unknown to his employers, Yeadon had booked Smile in to record at Pye and along with Geoff Calvar, a disc cutting engineer, they recorded two songs, 'Step On Me' and 'Polar Bar' and copied them on to acetate.

Terry Yeadon explained to Brian May that he was establishing a new studio complex in Wembley called De Lane Lea and needed a band to test the equipment. The complex comprised three adjoining studios and he was anxious to discover whether there was a bleed of sound from one to the other. They had even fired blanks from a shotgun to see if the separate desks detected the sound, but a live, loud rock group was far more suited to do the job.

Within days of their meeting, Queen were having free use of innovative studio technology. They were allowed to use the largest studio, which could hold up to 120 musicians, and a bank of Marshall stacks was hired to crank up the power. Aside from the clarity and power the studio supplied to Queen's music, De Lane Lea was virtually a music business thoroughfare: it was a workshop for emerging talent, from sound engineering to management.

With members as garrulous, confident and personable as Freddie Mercury and Roger Taylor, it was obvious that they would use the opportunity to make new contacts, and during their time in the studio they met their future production collaborators, John Anthony and Roy Thomas-Baker. John Anthony remembered Brian May and Roger Taylor from their days in Smile. Both he and Thomas-Baker said they would recommend the band to Barry and Norman Sheffield, the owners of Trident Studios in Soho, who were looking to become involved with promising new acts.

Queen spent long hours at De Lane Lea with the in-house producer Louie Austin. They had to work around the whims of artists whose recording was funded by record labels, and it often meant that sessions lasted deep into the night. Queen made no compromise to their standing as studio 'practice' band and were fastidious in their approach to recording. "They were very fussy," said Louie Austin. "The songs were done one by one. They would carry on until they thought it was right. It sometimes took a very long time but they put up with so much shit too, during that time." Queen recorded four of their own songs at the studio - 'Liar', 'Keep Yourself Alive', 'The Night Comes Down' and 'Jesus'. They had persevered with their song writing throughout the year and the live set also boasted additional original songs like 'Procession', 'Father To Son', and 'Ogre Battle'.

During the De Lane Lea sessions the band developed a manifesto on song writing which was to remain steadfast throughout most of their career. During a discussion about the author of the track 'Liar', Freddie announced, with his usual imperiousness, that he considered the 'writer' of a song to be the person who had contributed the lyric. It was a highly simplistic and flawed pronouncement but was generally accepted by the others, possibly as an endorsement and appeasement to Freddie's greater songwriting skill.

For the purposes of assessing what each contributor should receive in terms of royalty payments, a song is generally divided into twelfths and the separate contributions roughly split, usually with the lyrics contributing six-twelfths, or a half of the total. Freddie's policy inevitably meant he would, as singer and [therefore] main lyricist, lay claim on the lion's share of the performance royalties accrued by Queen, an immense sum which would later run to many millions. Brian May followed Freddie in terms of songwriting credits but Roger Taylor and John Deacon were left way behind. The others received an equal share of mechanical royalties which are paid per performer per record sold, but until May, Taylor and Deacon wrote hit songs themselves in their entirety they would accumulate wealth at a notably slower pace than Freddie.

The various bodies protecting the interests of Queen have remained mute on this potentially divisive situation, though there was brief reference made to it in the group's official biography. In it Freddie conceded that, "The rule almost certainly discouraged us from co-operating on lyrics for a long time, and started a trend towards separateness in song-producing, which was acute at the time of the Munich records [those made in the late Seventies and early Eighties]."

Songwriting credits provide fascinating insights into the power base of any group, and within Queen, one of rock's greatest cabals, it is, as always, divulged by the names in small print in brackets. Freddie's tactic of effectively prohibiting co-written songs meant that for the others to earn a publishing royalty it was necessary to include complete songs written by an individual group member on each LP. A brief perusal of Queen's albums until the final two, reveals that Roger Taylor and John Deacon rarely contributed more than two songs per album, (on the first two Deacon received no credits at all). They might simply have been less prolific than Freddie Mercury and Brian May, but it still implies more than an element of tokenism: though this must be placed in context with Freddie's songwriting prowess since hit songs like 'You're My Best Friend', 'Another One Bites The Dust', 'I Want To Break Free', 'Radio Ga Ga' and 'A Kind Of Magic' - all by either John Deacon or Roger Taylor - could hardly be considered 'token' efforts in terms of their musical vintage.

The brief discussion held at De Lane Lea in the winter of 1971 might have shaped their song writing strategy thereafter, but it is noteworthy that the twenty-two songs on their last two albums, 'Innuendo' and 'The Miracle', were ascribed to all four members of the group (aside from 'All God's People' which was credited to Queen and Mike Moran). This would suggest a compromise had been reached; the move would certainly partially address a lopsided balance of royalties if the main songwriter of a band were to die and a portion of the group's legacy was directed outside the band to satisfy the wishes of his estate.

The sessions at De Lane Lea provided Queen with a rare luxury since it allowed them to realise their own 'sound' almost immediately. Most groups have to contend with scratchy, thwarted demos for years before they are able to properly capture the sound that exists in their collective heads; sometimes, whether through incompetence or the wrong choice of producer or studio, artists never actually batten down on to tape what they consider to be their true sound. Queen, in contrast, though unsigned and unfancied, had a demo tape that summarised their sound precisely - power, a certain complexity of arrangement, intricate harmonies, and a fair smattering of melody.

The tape appeared to vitalise the band members and dispel some of their jittery reticence about a life devoted solely to rock'n'roll. Roger Taylor, whose commitment to anything outside the group was always cursory, left the stall on Kensington Market he had been running with Freddie. Alan Mair, the owner of a nearby shoe stall, took over and ran it with Freddie for a few more months. Brian May had also started to recognise the dilemma between his academic and musical side. He spoke increasingly to lecturers about his love of music and made it clear he would no longer be part of study trips to Tenerife. In a sudden change of tact, however, Brian May announced in November 1971 that he had found a full-time job, teaching at Stockwell Manor School, a large comprehensive in Brixton, south London. Whether he accepted the position through parental pressure or to earn himself some desperately needed cash is unknown, though it was to last less than a year.

Queen closed 1971 with another incongruous booking, at the London Rugby Club on New Year's Eve. They were still securing concerts from supportive friends putting the word around but there was at least a tiny clique in the music business who had seen and heard Queen and were prepared to make tentative endorsements. Ken Testi was the first to pledge himself to the cause and he worked tirelessly on their behalf. For a short period early in 1972 he shared a flat in London with Paul Conroy (now managing director of Virgin Records) and Lyndsay Brown. They were both booking acts for a concert agency, The Red Bus Company, based in Wardour Street, Soho. "I hassled them for gigs mercilessly," says Testi. "I gave them a demo tape of Queen and asked them to listen to it properly. They retired to the bedroom and when they re-emerged they said it was a good piece of work but the last thing the world needed was another Led Zeppelin. I agreed, because I didn't think they were another Led Zeppelin." They still offered Queen a support spot at King's College Hospital in Denmark Street on March 10, 1972, for which they received a fee of £20. It was a distinct improvement on Queen's first show of 1972, an appearance at Bedford College on January 28 organised by John Deacon which attracted just six paying customers.

Paul Conroy recognised Ken Testi's zeal for Queen, and arranged an appointment for him with Tony Stratton-Smith, the ebullient owner of Charisma Records. Stratton-Smith had built up a creditable reputation, chiefly for his unstinting devotion to the acts he signed, among them Genesis and Lindisfarne. From Charisma's small office in Dean Street he had conducted a fine campaign for 'Trespass', the first album Genesis recorded for Charisma, with a noted personal touch.

Tony Stratton-Smith liked Queen and offered them an advance of £20,000, an extremely reasonable sum, but they were concerned they were not his first love. "They were worried that they would be identified as second string on a small label," said Ken Testi. "Queen would have had a lot of personal support from the staff there, but they felt resources were limited. It wasn't a bad offer, but it came at a time when some bands' advances had been in telephone numbers. CBS had been paying out monstrous amounts."

Queen seemed to adopt a bizarre logic to Charisma's offer. Although recognising Stratton-Smith as 'an honest guy' and his offer as fairly generous, they decided to 'bank' it in the sense of using it to lever more money and commitment from other labels. "I felt relieved that there was a deal there but on the other hand, if there was one deal there ought to be another," said Ken. "I understood the band's reasons for turning it down. It all seemed great fun at the time, but I was slightly bemused by their lack of commitment to an action plan."

By early 1972 Ken Testi, along with the band and John Harris, had formed what he dubbed 'a council of war' - his own term for the tight unit they had become. It had not occurred to him to seek a formal arrangement but Queen began to make overtures that he should. Unfortunately for both parties, Queen's semi-formal approach was poorly timed for Ken Testi. The lease was about to expire on his Fulham flat, and his parents were splitting up; he felt it right he should return to Merseyside and offer financial and practical support to his mother. So, during the crucial early days of Queen, when they were set to become ensnared in an industry about which they knew very little, they were without an important ally. Ken Testi could only watch from afar, selling carpets in a high street store in Widnes. He recognised the nascent brilliance of Queen, knew where it was heading, but also understood that his role thereafter would be peripheral.

Before leaving London, Testi had witnessed the band's growing involvement with Norman and Barry Sheffield. Their Trident studios had renowned Triad mixing desks, and the set-up was regarded as one of the best in the UK. It was used extensively by leading players like David Bowie and Elton John, and the recording team within its portals were developing their own distinctive sound.

At this time Freddie Mercury had an extremely small record collection which he stored horizontally in a drawer at his flat. It was no more than a dozen albums including Liza Minelli's 'Cabaret', 'SF Sorrow' by The Pretty Things, which he heralded as the first rock opera, 'Tommy' by The Who, and various records by Led Zeppelin, The Beatles and David Bowie – a huge influence on both Freddie and Roger Taylor from his early acoustic shows onwards. In many ways, the grand, powerful production techniques developed at Trident crystallised Freddie's record collection and his own personal vision of Queen. It was imperative that he and his group record there and Ken Testi feels Freddie might have manipulated fate to make it happen.

For some time Freddie had cruised the King's Road and the streets around it in the fashionable borough of Kensington and Chelsea. It was little more than a pose, but he would parade in his fineries and search out luminaries from the pop, and to a lesser extent, art world. He paid particular attention to his appearance on Saturdays and would sometimes spend the whole afternoon promenading along Kensington High Street, leaving his stall in someone else's custody. Ken Testi believes that for some time Freddie had purposely hoped to meet John Anthony, the young producer forging a name for himself at Trident who had previously worked with Smile and passed through De Lane Lea while Queen were recording at the studio. "I am sure there was some kind of conspiracy," Testi maintains. "Freddie would spend ages dressing himself up and when I asked him why he did it he would say, 'You never know who you might meet'."

He did, indeed, meet John Anthony and after Freddie plied him with tales of his band's distinctive talent, Queen were invited to Anthony's flat to talk further. The producer invited his employers, the Sheffields, to see Queen at a show at Forest Hill Hospital on March 24 and the band put in an excellent performance. Queen, and Ken Testi, were requested to meet formally with Trident at the earliest opportunity.

The mood at their first meeting was unlike any previous experience for Queen. It was carried out with an almost exclusive emphasis on business arrangements rather than music. "They were two quite imposing fellows," said Ken Testi. "They explained they were forming a production company. They already had the studio, so in a way they were simply moving up the food chain. They were talking in telephone numbers which Queen found attractive. What I don't think the band realised at the time was that they would be part of a package involving two other acts. Trident didn't say anything about this package at the time, it was some way down the line when they found out about it. To me, it all looked like the grey men in suits. It was a commodity as far as the Sheffields were concerned. Put it this way, there wasn't a lot of humour in the room."

Queen took a great deal of time before actually signing to Trident – nearly eight months, a period during which they did not play a single concert. In hindsight, it is difficult to understand the delay since Ken Testi cannot remember any lawyers being consulted. It would seem the band were still soliciting interest from other quarters and were scrutinising the small print themselves. The deliberation certainly did not lead to a contract which favoured the group in any unique way; in fact, the band and subsequent advisors later considered it a very poor contract. Freddie Mercury was certainly lucid about the Queen-Trident partnership once it had been dissolved some years afterwards: "As far as Queen are concerned our old management is deceased. They cease to exist in any capacity with us whatsoever. One leaves them behind like one leaves excreta. We feel so relieved."

Trident was in a much stronger bargaining position than Queen. Apart from being an established and substantial force on the music scene, Trident Audio

Services had an unparalleled inducement to offer a fledgling group – a deal which would provide access to studio facilities out of reach even to most groups already signed to major labels. As a taster of Trident's opulence, Queen were immediately supplied with a new public address system and each were bought new instruments, apart from Brian May who said he was quite happy with the Red Special.

The first album was the most important for any act, even more so in the case of a fastidious, serious-minded band like Queen. It was the culmination of years of dedication and hitherto abstract creativity. It was the statement, the branding; put simply, the artistic birth. Trident Studios would yield the most expansive, accomplished début possible for Queen and it would seem the allure was perhaps too great.

Queen insisted on separate sub-contracts covering publishing, management and recording but this appeared to have been largely a cosmetic exercise. In plain terms Trident Audio Services planned to colonise Queen. In several shrewd, but perfectly legal moves, Trident adopted the roles and functions normally served by several different parties. It would record the band, produce them, manage them, sub-publish them, and secure them a record deal. This would, of course, invoke several conflicts of interest, but it was not a particularly unique approach in an insidiously dubious business.

The most bizarre twist was Trident's apparent plan to present Queen along with two other acts as a 'package deal', though there is some confusion as to whether this was ever more than an impertinently ambitious idea. Any such package may not have needed to be related explicitly in the contract, but by today's legal precepts, which tend to draw greater sanction for the artist, it might be construed as a restraint of trade: an artist's success or failure should not depend on the fortunes of a completely unconnected act which just happens to share the same contract space.

Much of Trident's philosophy had been formed by an experienced music business operator, Jack Nelson. An American, Nelson, had served his apprenticeship in his home country which was more than a few steps ahead of the UK in its business manoeuvres. He had formed Blue Thumb in the US, one of the first independent production companies. Ultimately, the dual stance made for greater control of the 'product' and greater financial returns. Since Nelson had galvanised the Sheffields' move along the 'food chain', it was perhaps obvious that they would encourage him to oversee the project.

Jack Nelson liked Queen's demo tape, and, to a lesser extent, the other two who were part of the supposed 'package' – Eugene Wallace and Mark Ashton. He agreed to move to London and place Queen with a business manager sympathetic to the band and the aims of Trident. He was astounded that others did not share his passion for Queen and after several rebuffs, he decided to become their manager himself; the idea was suggested to him by another American manager, Dee Anthony, who had managed the crooner Tony Bennett and, more recently, Joe Cocker. Anthony rejected Queen because he was about to manage Humble Pie, a band, he promised, who would eventually be much bigger than Queen.

It would have suited Trident if a record label had offered to fund Queen's recordings, but after EMI among several others turned them down, it fell upon Trident to offer its own studio to the band. Queen were possibly surprised to discover that they were not top priority within the Trident empire. They were told that their recording sessions would take place during 'down time' when others had finished early, postponed or cancelled. Queen, though potentially set to earn Trident vast sums of money, were placed in the undignified position of having to squeeze their sessions in around paying guests like David Bowie, Elton John and a variety of perpetual unknowns. "They would call us up and say David Bowie had finished a few hours early, so we had from 3 am to 7 am when the cleaners came in," said Brian May. "A lot of it was done that way. There were a few full days but mainly bits and pieces."

On one occasion, while they were lingering at the studio they were invited by a producer, Robin Cable, to provide backing on a cover of a Phil Spector song, 'I Can Hear Music', a version of which recorded by The Beach Boys had reached number 10 in March 1969. Freddie sang while Brian May and Roger Deacon supplied the instrumentation and vocal harmonies. They each received a small session fee but their cooperation had been naïve since they held no control over the finished tapes. The song was released a year later as a single by EMI and designed as a spoof of Gary Glitter under the name of Larry Lurex. The joke misfired when DJs, solemnly loyal to Gary Glitter, refused to mention or play the record. It sold only a handful of copies and disappeared without trace until its re-release as a collectors' item many years later. Rather unfortunately for Queen, it will forever remain a blemish on their recorded canon because, technically at least, it was their first record release.

Brian May had spent nearly a year teaching at Stockwell Manor while he worked simultaneously on his PhD. The manuscript for his thesis had been drafted but not typed when he finally conceded that he should commit himself solely to music. Professors at Imperial College who had read the thesis considered it strong enough to earn him a doctorate, through which he would have become Dr Brian May. At Stockwell Manor he was taken to task by maths teacher, Mr Simon, who questioned the sense of leaving the teaching profession. He was asked to consider the 'prospects, security and pension' of the job.

At the end of September 1972 Trident put the members of Queen on a weekly wage of £20. It was a magnanimous move because the band did not officially sign the contract until several weeks later. The wage coincided with Roger Taylor graduating from North London Polytechnic with a degree in biology and John Deacon with a first in electronics from London University.

New Album, Old News

Chapter X

Queen

The tracks which formed Queen's début album were recorded almost in their entirety when they signed formally to Trident in November 1972. It had been a peculiar way to design an album, but considering the irregular sessions and constantly changing studio personnel, everyone agreed the songs had a coherence which camouflaged the erratic nature of the recording. Roy Thomas-Baker and John Anthony, as producers, had shown a degree of allegiance to Queen and insisted that they be granted more time for mixing after Trident wanted to put a deadline on the project. Mike Stone, the studio's trainee sound engineer, had found Queen exemplary professionals despite the shoddy working arrangement. "That first album was completely different to anything else I had been doing," said Mike Stone. "The remixes took ages and ages, and the band all seemed such perfectionists that every little squeak had to be just right. It was quite nerve racking working with a born superstar [Freddie Mercury] on the first major work I had engineered."

Trident, Jack Nelson specifically, had been 'talking up' Queen since the spring of 1972 but his efforts through the summer had brought scant response. In theory it should have been an appealing project for record companies because they could actually hear the whole album brilliantly recorded; it was a much smaller risk than the usual procedure of hearing a rough demo tape and trusting (and paying for) an act to repeat and enhance the material in a better studio.

While they were ensconced in the studio, Queen were deflected away from Trident's business dealings but when the recording had finished they soon became frustrated by the inactivity. They grew suspicious and word filtered through that they were being touted as a package to music publishers and record companies with two other acts, Eugene Wallace and Mark Ashton. "Unfortunately they were selling us as part of a package of their production company and they wanted the package accepted as a whole," said Brian May in a magazine interview. Freddie Mercury contacted Ken Testi and told him of their suspicions. "They had a feeling that they would be hanging around for ever waiting for the record to be released," said Testi.

It is unclear whether Trident initially hoped to secure a package deal for the trio, and then altered its strategy when it realised the 'all or nothing' was too daunting for most companies. Either way, the first unequivocal patronage for Trident's deal came from the music publisher, B. Feldman and Co., which did, in fact, take on all three acts as a package. Feldman's would turn out to be a crucial but largely uncelebrated player in the fortunes of Queen. While others hesitated and continued to do so, its staff adopted Queen with rare warmth and fervour.

Feldman's, like all old style music publishers, was originally formed to oversee the copyright of sheet music. They printed the sheet music to popular songs, promoted it to shops, and collected a percentage, usually the statutory rate of six and a quarter per cent; the remainder was paid as a royalty to the songwriter. Established at the beginning of the century, B. Feldman and Co. was a respected publishing house, owning the rights to thousands of songs including standards like 'It's A Long Way To Tipperary', 'Who's Sorry Now?' and the songs of the jazz innovator Jelly Roll Morton.

In the mid-Fifties the role of the music publisher changed dramatically, switching from the traditional marketing of printed sheet music to acting as a collection agency for sums owed on song copyrights it owned or administered. By the late Sixties and early Seventies, and the spread of rock radio, they acted as agents for songwriters, collecting the royalties they were due each time one of their songs was broadcast. Feldman's had a strong roster, it secured the UK rights to leading artists like Bob Dylan, The Hollies, and The Searchers, and continued its enterprising policy into the Seventies with bands like Wishbone Ash and Deep Purple.

While many publishers had previously been chiefly administrative bodies, with a somewhat sedentary reputation, they became pro-active in the Sixties and Seventies, and this was very much to Queen's benefit. Like record companies, and often in union with them, they had formed an A&R role. There was an expansive market in radio, television and films and it consumed vast amounts of new material, generating untold wealth in royalties. Songwriters, and the groups with whom they performed, were coveted like never before.

In the late summer of 1972 Jack Nelson had contacted Feldman's with a view to a joint deal with Trident. Trident would supply three acts - Queen, Mark Ashton (under the guise of his group, Headstone) and Eugene Wallace - and together they would place the trio with a record company as soon as possible. Ronnie Beck, the managing director of Feldman's, had already seen Queen perform live, in December 1971 at Epsom Swimming Baths, Surrey, where he thought they were 'absolutely fantastic'.

Phil Reed, a plugger for Feldman's, vividly recalls the first formal meeting between Jack Nelson and Ronnie Beck at Feldman's headquarters in Dean Street, Soho. "I could hear the tape playing in Ronnie's office," he said. "It was 'Keep Yourself Alive' and I knew straight away that it was something special. I went in as soon as Jack had gone and asked him who the band were, I'd never heard of Queen before. Queen became a real labour of love for Ronnie, they did for all of us really. They got a lot of attention and promotion from us."

Feldman's paid Queen an advance of £2,000 for the global publishing rights for the next three years. It was probably the most lucrative piece of business Ronnie Beck had ever undertaken; he believes Queen brought in £500,000 in royalties within six months of releasing their first album, though this would appear to be a somewhat liberal estimate.

The other two acts, although undoubtedly secondary to Queen, were also admired within Feldman's; they certainly weren't perceived as makeweight or passengers in the deal. Mark Ashton had previously drummed with Rare Bird and had been a founding member along with Steve Gould, Graham Field and Dave Kaffinetti, each of them stalwarts of the same Middlesex scene which had propelled Brian May. Headstone were fundamentally Rare Bird under a different name and with a heavier sound. Mark Ashton had moved on to guitar and the only musician not to make the transition from the original band was Graham Field. Eugene Wallace was an emotive Irish singer in the mode of Joe Cocker. It seemed an enticing trio of acts, each of them modern, ingenious in their own way, and with commercial potential.

The three acts received equal attention, but most of the twenty-five-strong staff at Feldman's believed Queen would attract most notice. They were amazed when a succession of record companies passed on them. "It was very frustrating," said Phil Reed. "Every one of us believed in the band but it was something people weren't prepared to gamble on. It wasn't as if we were asking for vast amounts of money as an advance. I always thought Queen were unique but everyone kept saying they sounded too much like Yes and Led Zeppelin, I couldn't see the comparison myself. We did the rounds everywhere but most of the major labels passed on them. We weren't going to give up though. We kept saying to ourselves, 'This band are amazing, why can't they get a record deal?'"

In November 1972 a showcase concert was arranged at The Pheasantry, a club in the King's Road, Chelsea. Both Trident and Feldman's had spent some weeks persuading music business associates to attend, all to no avail. The public address system arrived late and the band's performance was unpolished, 'scruffy around the edges', as Norman Sheffield later commented. Phil Reed attended and felt a great sympathy for the band. "Not one A&R guy turned up. It was really a disco place and once the disco had stopped and Queen went on everyone went to the bar. Once Queen started virtually everyone had left the room. I remember me and Ronnie Beck were sat there unable to believe it. There was only a few of the band's friends left," he said.

Queen's last show of 1972, and one of only five during the whole year, was at The Marquee Club on December 20. Ronnie Beck was a good friend of John Sherry, a promoter who regularly booked bands into The Marquee, and he kindly agreed to find Queen the occasional gig. Their performance and the audience response was an improvement on The Pheasantry, but it brought them no closer to a record deal, not in the UK at least. Ronnie Beck, whose resolution was merely focused by the industry's apathy, had invited Jac Holtzman, the managing director of Elektra Records, to the show and afterwards Holtzman agreed to sign the band for the US. Queen were now part of a roster boasting The Doors and Love on a credible American label which was trying to re-establish itself in the Seventies.

Ronnie Beck is categoric that Trident did not offer Queen as part of a package deal, and that there was no constraint on where he placed the three acts he had purchased for Feldman's. "It definitely wasn't a package," he insists. "I went to different record companies with each artist; you don't take Vera Lynn to a rock concert do you? Eugene Wallace was a brilliant singer and I got him a deal in America with United Artists, while we went with Elektra for Queen." Beck does not share the jaundiced view of Trident held later by Queen, and he worked closely with the company during many crucial negotiations. "They had spent an awful lot of their own money and time on Queen. The demo tapes we were hauling around had been very expensive to make. The Sheffield brothers were OK. Two good lads. They ran one of the best studios in London and a lot of successful bands used it. They paid their bills and were sharp and clever." Brian May, many years after the ties were severed, also recognised the importance of Trident's galvanising role: "We obviously owe some of our success to Trident - they got us making records and hits, for instance," he said.

In Jack Nelson, Jac Holtzman, Feldman's and Trident, Queen had some influential players in their camp, and yet even with a sparkling demo tape they could not find a record deal in the UK. They were seeking a substantial advance, but the industry's indifference was uncanny, almost as if a negative whisper had been circulated about the band. "It was frustrating when I kept getting this, 'I'll let you know' response," said Beck. "I phoned EMI Records and they kept saying their A&R guy was busy, or out at some meeting. It was different outside the UK. I took the tape to Germany and they were jumping up and down about it." The band, to their credit, kept their nerve during this disheartening period. "They were patient," notes Phil Reed. "They believed it would happen for them. They knew how good they were. They knew what they were doing and had a big interest in everything that was going on. They were managed at the time but they could have managed themselves, they were something different from most bands."

A catalyst in moving Queen towards a record deal was their Radio 1 session recorded in February 1973. Still unknown outside a few London venues and music business gossip, it was a coup when Phil Reed persuaded producer Bernie Andrews to record an unsigned group. Queen laid down four songs on February 5 at Langham One studio, across the road from Broadcasting House in Portland Place. Phil Etchell engineered the raw versions of 'My Fairy King', 'Keep Yourself Alive', 'Liar' and the original Smile song, 'Doing Alright'. The session was broadcast on John Peel's *Sounds Of The Seventies* programme ten days later. The hour long show was aired at 6 pm throughout the week with different DJs each night and was the BBC's substantial pledge to inventive new music.

Feldman's, meanwhile, was subject to a takeover by EMI Music Publishing which was the UK's largest music publishing concern at the time. Feldman's had already amalgamated with two other houses, Robbins Music Ltd and Francis, Day and Hunter Ltd, and had started to trade as Affiliated Music when EMI pounced. Its staff were moved to the headquarters of EMI Publishing in Denmark Place and initially, at least, they were told they would continue to handle existing Feldman clients.

It was pure coincidence that Queen soon found themselves signed to both EMI Music Publishing and EMI Records. There had been an indeterminate relationship between Queen and EMI Records during most of 1972 and the early part of 1973. EMI's head of A&R, Joop Visser, was tacitly a fan of the group, but he felt they needed to improve their live show and he was apprehensive of their financial demands.

Joop Visser, a Dutchman who had worked for EMI in his home country and BASF in Germany, had moved to the UK in 1972. He was beginning to collect a series of laudable rock groups with a commercial bent like Be Bop Deluxe, Cockney Rebel, Pilot and Gonzalez. "I heard the half-finished tapes Queen had done at the studio," said Visser. "I thought it had something good going for it. I thought Queen were a heavy group. Deep Purple had fallen apart and we needed something in that direction. I went to see them rehearsing in a gymnasium at Kingston-Upon-Thames but they were terrible." He met the members of Queen and was left nonplussed: "They didn't strike me as anything special. I did not fall flat on my arse about their personalities. I thought they were a bit withdrawn. I saw a lot more of the other groups I signed and got on with them better."

Ronnie Beck continued to ply Visser and along with several members of EMI's staff he had attended the showcase at the Marquee. "Again, I didn't think the band was too together and the response from most of the staff was that they weren't too hot," Visser notes. "For me, it was only after they toured with Mott The Hoople that they really got it together, and I mean got it frighteningly together. They scared Mott The Hoople at the end of that tour because they were stealing the shows."

Perhaps chiefly out of respect for Ronnie Beck, whom Joop Visser considered 'one of the most adventurous publishers', he entered preliminary contract negotiations.

"I remember that at the time, for an unknown band, they wanted a substantial advance, it was well into five figures," said Visser. "It was a production deal and I immediately decided it was too much money for me to sanction, not that I didn't think they were worth it."

It was against these 'skirmishes and vague rumblings' (as Joop Visser termed the prevailing relationship between EMI Records and Queen) that Ronnie Beck finally secured a record deal. It was moved to completion early in 1973 at the music industry's main annual trade fair, MIDEM, held in the south of France. Ronnie Beck played the Queen tape to EMI Records' A&R executive Roy Featherstone and he was impressed, mainly with the track 'Liar'. "I had chased Roy around all bloody week," Beck recalled. "I'd played it to various other people and was thinking, 'For Christ's sake something's got to happen soon.' I met up with Roy in the hall at the hotel where publishers were running around. I sat him down and he liked it. It seemed odd doing a deal all that way from home when we could have got on a bus in London and we were only twenty minutes away from each other's office."

A record deal, however, is not a panacea, but merely another fight for a band, a different kind of fight. There is more money around, especially when signed to a corporate monolith like EMI, but there are also more meetings and minutes, deferments and disagreements, bureaucracy and regimen, errors and anxiety. It suddenly and understandably becomes serious – someone might lose their job; that serious. Bands, or more usually their forceful representatives, have to make themselves a priority within the record company. And they have to comply with budgets, shake hands with people they'd rather write sneering songs about. It's now a career and this isn't rock'n'roll, this is cost accounting. It has its own vocabulary. A record is product. Stock is a quantity of records. A plan is a schedule. A three-hour skive is a meeting. An attitude problem is a band with its own ideas. Every artist has gone through this mercantile mangle, even the protest singers who told us capitalism was profane, when their very existence depended on it.

Queen embarked upon it in the spring of 1973 when they signed finally to EMI Records after nearly a year of shadow play. The advance, though never formally revealed, was clearly substantial and this, as much as their obvious musical promise, guaranteed that they took a fairly high precedence within the company. Basically, to ensure the advance was recouped, EMI had to do everything within its power to sell Queen's records. As there was already a batch of songs recorded, the time span between signing the recording contract and releasing a record was unusually short, just a few months.

John Deacon, on one of his infrequent trips back to Oadby, played a pre-release tape of 'Keep Yourself Alive' to his former colleague in The Opposition, Dave Williams: "I remember he turned up with this demo. He was driving a massive old Rover car at the time. I thought the song was really good, I distinctly remember saying that the guitar playing was really good, nearly as good as Ritchie Blackmore. We were all into Deep Purple in a big way and I thought this was a great compliment, but John said he wasn't sure how Brian would respond to this!"

Before he returned to London, John Deacon asked Dave Williams to carry out a special favour. To activate sales of Queen's début album, he asked him to travel around Leicester pre-ordering it from shops. "I started a bit later than I should," he said. "It must have already been released, because everywhere I went I was told it was sold out. I was a bit surprised because I didn't think many people had heard of Queen. I was really proud of John."

Another friend John Deacon invariably tracked down in Oadby was Nigel Bullen, the former drummer with The Opposition. He also had an early introduction to the music of Queen when John Deacon arrived with an advance tape of the first album. Both Nigel Bullen and his wife Ruth felt they already knew of Queen's importance to John, but they were astonished by his white hot intensity. Before the evening was finished John Deacon was talking of Queen's ten-year plan and going into great detail about future world tours; it all seemed extremely imaginative, though they didn't mention it. "His personality is usually quiet and reserved but he was the most animated I have ever seen him that night," said Ruth Bullen. "He spent hours talking about Queen, constantly playing the album through. It was all done so intelligently, with such microscopic detail. He was talking about other bands and how they'd been ripped off and how everything had to be so well organised from the very beginning."

'Keep Yourself Alive', Queen's first single (discounting the Larry Lurex episode), was released on July 6, 1973. It was the band's first introduction to the conflicting nature of critical response. *Record Mirror* said it was 'a raucous, well built single,' but *Melody Maker* countered that it 'lacked originality'. Radio 1 did not like the record. On five separate occasions EMI's pluggers attempted to secure it space on the play list but were rebuffed every time. Word came through that the record 'took too long to happen' and Queen vowed that their next single would be designed specifically to have immediate impact. Only Alan Freeman, whose Radio 1 programme fell outside the play list format, gave it airtime. 'Keep Yourself Alive' did not chart, the only one of 42 in Queen's lifespan to suffer this ignominy.

The staff at EMI soon realised that the members of Queen had an extraordinary dedication to the cause. Most bands had a nonchalant attitude towards the finer points of presentation and marketing but Queen were downright fanatical. They were seldom away from EMI's offices and insisted that they sanctioned every creative decision. They had clear ideas of how they wished to present themselves and EMI granted them a fair degree of autonomy.

Doug Puddifoot, a friend of Roger Taylor's, took Queen's first ever publicity shots in Freddie's flat, among the fringed lamp shades and artefacts collected at Kensington Market. The original plan for the album sleeve was to have the band framed in an oval-shaped photograph with a sepia finish, essentially a pastiche of Victoriana. Brian May had the superior idea of showing Freddie in suitably heroic pose bathed in light. The sleeve brilliantly captured Queen's magnetism - a confounding union of light and dark, heroism and understatement. The early suggestions for an album title were less germane. Roger Taylor wanted 'Top Fax, Pix and Info' and there was an entreaty for 'Deary Me', one of the regular laments of Roy Thomas-Baker. Eventually, following the trend of the times, they decided to name the album after the band.

In the haphazard fashion typical of record companies, EMI sent a white label copy of the album to BBC television but forget to include any information about it, not even the name of the group. Mike Appleton, the producer of *The Old Grey Whistle Test*, stumbled upon it and both he and the programme's presenter, Bob Harris, were anxious to learn more. They decided to play the opening track,

'Keep Yourself Alive', without knowing the band's identity. On July 24 a monochrome cartoon was screened to accompany the music; this was not a particularly unique move because the programme predated the era of the promotional video.

Both Trident and EMI made the *Whistle Test* team aware of the band's name within hours of the broadcast and Bob Harris reinforced his support for the group by booking them to record a session for his Radio 1 programme. On July 25 they were back at the famous Langham One studio, this time with producer Jeff Griffin, where they recorded versions of 'See What A Fool I've Been', 'Liar', 'Son And Daughter' and 'Keep Yourself Alive'. "They were so dynamic," said Bob Harris. "I put on the opening track of the album and thought, 'Wow'. The music was so appealing, it didn't seem contrived or manipulated, it was really, really refreshing."

Bob Harris, along with another Radio 1 DJ, Anne Nightingale, became an ally of the group, and a much valued early supporter. The band often showed their appreciation; he was sent a personal letter, signed by all four members in the parcel containing their second album. He was privy to several insights into the band – the unique partnership of disparate personalities, the attachment to their fans, the extravagant indulgence, and, some time later, their explicit business dealings. "Whenever they played in the studio at the *Whistle Test* I could feel the warmth generated by the audience to the band," he said. "One of my lasting memories is being at the side of the stage while Queen performed and feeling the glow from the audience. I think of all the other performers we had on, only Elton John could draw on the same affection."

Bob Harris remained a loyal supporter of Queen throughout the decade. He compèred the massive open air show at Hyde Park in September 1976 and the concert at the New London Theatre in October 1977 which was filmed for the video of 'We Are The Champions'. As a fan, friend, respected DJ and experienced broadcaster, he was the natural choice to assemble footage for an official Queen documentary.

He was invited to film the band at close quarters, mainly during their American tour of 1978. Queen planned to later sell the film to television companies throughout the world. Initially, the project went splendidly. He recorded lengthy interviews with each band member and was pleased by their candidness. The interview with Freddie was filmed in his garden, lasted three hours and, according to Harris, was 'a lovely piece'. Queen placed no restraint on the filming and said they would be happy to input purely creative ideas; collages, slow motion shots etc.

The filming provided Harris with an unusually close inspection of Queen off-guard and he largely approved of the view. He became especially close to Roger Taylor and they went on a three-day binge in Las Vegas where they vowed to have at least one drink in every bar and hotel. "It was the era of self indulgence," he said. "They each had their own limo and sometimes it would have been easier to walk to the venues from the hotels but that wasn't Queen's style. Freddie was theatrical but not hostile or aggressive. They were all very courteous. I cannot remember a single moment when there was an atmosphere."

Back in London, the editing of the film took much longer than expected. There were literally hundreds of hours of footage to sift through and Harris began to have misgivings about the assignment. "I think I'd bit off more than I could chew," he said. "I tried to do it with the film crew from the *Whistle Test* but we were making slow progress and it was a very time consuming project."

The enterprise ended abruptly when two burly men visited the editing studio, claimed they were from Queen's management, and confiscated all the reels of tape. "It was quite heavy I suppose," he said. "We didn't have chance to say too much. It was terribly frustrating that it should come to a complete stop like that. It was just cut off. Clearly they must have been frustrated at it taking such a long time but it might have been more appropriate to discuss it and decide what to do."

Bob Harris tried to make contact with Queen and their representatives but his messages were not returned, in fact it was several years before his relations with the band were restored: "All of a sudden it brought to an end the social life we had together. I felt very disappointed on a personal level, but there was no hostility or axe to grind between me and the band. It was just a shame to see friendships I was enjoying coming to nothing."

Three years later there was a small expression of conciliation when Bob Harris was in a restaurant with the singer Kiki Dee. Freddie Mercury was dining at another table and sent over a bottle of champagne. Also, when Radio 1 carried a retrospective piece on *The Old Grey Whistle Test*, Brian May greeted Bob Harris with a hug in the radio station. The documentary - what happened to the footage and Queen's bizarre stratagem - was never mentioned.

Some years later, Queen had a similar quarrel with another Radio 1 DJ who had offered essential early support, John Peel. After a video of 'Radio Ga Ga', complete with hundreds of people in uniforms clapping in syncopation, had been screened on *Top Of The Pops*, Peel, who was presenting the programme, commented that it reminded him of a Nuremburg rally. It was a crude response, but made flippantly and without real malevolence. Roger Taylor, the writer of the song, reacted strongly when it might have been more diplomatic to ignore the remark. "They threatened to have me done over or something, but I've not seen them since," said John Peel.

EMI invested heavily in the promotion of Queen's début album, paying for in-store displays at record shops and taking out extensive newspaper advertising. Initially at least it did not sell particularly well and for a good while the marketing expenditure surpassed the income from sales. Inevitably this led to claims of hype, but this was a routine mewl from an industry consumed by envy.

By the time it was released the album was really old news as far as Queen were concerned. Most of the tracks had an antecedence from years before and the delay in finding a record deal meant the public representation of Queen was out of kilter with the reality; they had written a number of new songs and felt their sound had evolved considerably. They were so exasperated that they included a telling sleeve note, claiming the album, '... represented at last something of what Queen music has been over the last three years...' It was a coded disclaimer, and Brian May later explained why they thought it necessary: "We were upset and felt that the record was old-fashioned by the time it came out. Lots of stuff had happened in the meantime, particularly David Bowie and Roxy Music, who were our sort of generation, but who had already made it, and we felt it would look like we were jumping on their bandwagon, whereas we'd actually had all that stuff in the can from a very long time before, and it was extremely frustrating."

Pretentious Even...

Chapter XI

Queen

The role of publicist was at its most crucial during the Seventies. Channels of exposure for new artists like videos, regional commercial radio stations and rock television programmes had still to be properly maximised, so the only real opportunities for new artists in particular came via Radio 1 and the all-powerful UK weekly music press. In 1973 *Melody Maker* was on a roll, occasionally selling as many as 200,000 copies a week, with *New Musical Express* not far behind. Unlike today, with its coverage marginalised, its circulation down to around 50,000 and its power diluted by competition, a positive story about a new act on *Melody Maker's* front page in the early Seventies was more or less guaranteed to push their album into the Top Ten.

It was therefore vitally important that Queen solicited support from the press and in August 1973 Jack Nelson enlisted the services of publicist Tony Brainsby, one of the most respected on the scene. His client base included Paul McCartney's new band Wings, Cat Stevens, Thin Lizzy, The Strawbs, Steeleye Span and Wizzard, and he was the consummate choice to drown the chorus of hype and actively 'break' the band.

Highly animated, Tony Brainsby was a bespectacled, copper-haired live-wire on the pop scene and invitations to parties at his Earl's Court home-cum-office in Edith Grove were much sought after. He was perpetually surrounded by attractive girls, many of whom worked for him, and stories circulated in the music business about one particular party at which a girl on LSD reposed naked in a bathtub filled with liquid jelly which set around her.

Brainsby was astounded by Queen's innate understanding of the business of promoting music. More usually much of his time was spent shaping a band's image but this aspect of his job was at least, in his words, 'half done' when he took on Queen. "They knew what their identity was, they had the logo, they knew how they wanted to look on pictures," he said. "They came out at a hippy time but they were the opposite of it. They were almost glam rock, they had elements of it, but it was on a higher, much more sophisticated level. Freddie already knew that he was a star and it was just a case of me helping Queen make their dreams come true that little bit quicker. As soon as I met Freddie I knew he was something very special... that the guy was a star. I have only had that feeling once or twice in my life."

A publicist's first task with a new client is to write a biography for release to the press. The 500 or so words have to epitomise the artist, in terms of both prose style and the detail either included or omitted. Tony Brainsby had two immediate 'angles' on which to base his narrative, and they were both to recur with monotonous regularity down the years. In short, Queen - unlike most rock bands - were highly intelligent chaps with university degrees (or the equivalent), and Brian May had made his own guitar from a fireplace.

Another singular feature of Queen was that they already had a certain 'buzz', a tentative ground swell of support. Usually Tony Brainsby had to create this for his clients but with Queen, "the buzz was there from the word go. They had an amazing following for what I thought was an unknown group. We immediately started getting phone calls from people who said they were fans, and some of them were in their thirties and forties. I remember thinking, 'How on earth has this happened?' They already had this aura about them."

Queen's early exposure came through the teen pin-up press. One of the first publications to carry a colour shot of their celestial features, colourful clothes and soft tresses was the girls' magazine *Jackie*. Queen, at this stage, had no qualms about where they were featured, but they were stringent over the release of pictures and information; it had to carry their official approval. Freddie Mercury was sensitive about his protruding teeth, and would scrutinise contact sheets to ensure no photographs were released showing them in a particularly bad light.

Mercury did some early press interviews but did not enjoy them and seemed to be the most hurt by negative press criticism. "Freddie was always very sensitive about the reviews," said Tony Brainsby. "He would read them through carefully and be bothered about something really small, like a full stop in the wrong place. Freddie was better at being seen, heard, but not known. I am sure that his not doing interviews made him more enigmatic, at least on a sub-conscious level, and he would have been aware of that. The others were happy to do them, so we only used Freddie when there was a new product or major tour to promote. We had hit records more or less from the word go so journalists were happy to speak to any member of the band. As long as they had a slice of the action they weren't really bothered that it wasn't Freddie in particular."

Queen quickly acquired a deep mistrust of the press, and it evolved to a paranoic level. Brian May's lament in a magazine article in 1983 summarised their basic viewpoint: "We have never really got on with the press and have a lot of enemies there... just about everyone in the press was against us, and quite blatantly so." Even so, it was May and Roger Taylor who would undertake most of the press interviews throughout Queen's career. Freddie Mercury was too sensitive about being misquoted, while John Deacon maintained an almost total disregard, possibly even contempt, for the press, and was seldom called upon at interview time.

Queen's early reviews were mixed, but they were no more pernicious or intolerant than those amassed by most bands of consequence. Queen were dispensing a vividly defined image and sound, and it was unlikely that critics would be ambiguous in their response. A recurring criticism of Queen was their earnest, po-faced attitude to themselves. Their reluctance to bear press censure (or, at its most extreme, contemptuous ridicule) with dignity only served to magnify this image of superciliousness. By the Eighties Queen had learned to relax and often mocked themselves with several videos based heavily on self parody. It helped to counter much of the earlier ponderous solemnity.

Tony Brainsby remained at Queen's side until shortly after the release of 'Bohemian Rhapsody'. He received a weekly retainer of about £20 from Trident and during his time with the band he gained a real insight. "I look back on those days fondly," said Brainsby. "The whole band gelled together perfectly, there wasn't a spare part. Freddie and Roger did their thing while John Deacon was solid, there, the equivalent of Bill Wyman in The Rolling Stones or John Entwistle in The Who. Roger Taylor was a party animal. Roger was so pretty and he handled it really well, he played it down rather than playing it up. I had no problems with Trident, their cheques didn't bounce. I was Queen's PR man so the business side didn't really have a lot to do with me. I still admired the band's strength to come through all that though."

Queen relinquished the services of Tony Brainsby when their deal with Trident ended in 1975. Their new manager, John Reid, had his own public relations staff and preferred them to handle Queen's press campaigns. "I worked with John Reid for a few weeks but it was bloody hard work," said Brainsby. "I was very much part of the old Queen – Trident, Jack Nelson and everything. I think John Reid wanted a clean sweep and I had no problem with that. The band tried to drag me through but John made life very difficult." Tony Brainsby returned to the fold briefly in 1978 to handle the band's notoriously flawed strategy on the double A-sided single 'Fat Bottomed Girls' and 'Bicycle Race'.

EMI appeared to agree with Queen that their released output was trailing behind their natural musical development. Instead of asking the group to promote their début album, which would have been the customary tactic, EMI allowed them to start work immediately on their next album. During the summer of 1973, just a few weeks after the first album's release, Queen were back in Trident studios laying down tracks for 'Queen II'. They no longer had to record during down time and had full use of the studio.

Queen's return to live performance was on September 13 at Golders Green Hippodrome in London. They had been invited to play by Radio 1 as part of its *In Concert* series. The show was recorded and broadcast a month later and gave a fitting showcase to Queen's efficacy in performance. The concert opened with a tape of an atmospheric piece of music before the band broke into 'Procession'. Freddie Mercury introduced the next track, 'Father To Son' with the address: "A word in your ear, from father to son". In their nail varnish, satin trousers and loose blouses, Queen were starting to form their own unique brand of delivery. The set was still somewhat leaden, two drum solos - in 'Liar' and 'Keep Yourself Alive' - for example, but their panache relieved even these unnecessary interludes.

In September 1973 Jack Nelson contacted an acquaintance of his, Bob Hirschmann, who was managing Mott The Hoople. A fellow American, Hirschmann was a former saxophone player who had once had a small part in a film starring Spencer Tracey. Mott The Hoople had been signed to Island Records for three years and established themselves as an anarchic and popular live attraction, but only lately had they enjoyed four Top Twenty hits, the first of which, 'All The Young Dudes', was written and produced by David Bowie the previous year. They were planning a UK tour taking in twenty prestigious venues and with their latest single, 'All The Way From Memphis', a Top Ten hit, the dates were almost sure to sell out. Queen, with one flop single behind them, were unlikely to boost ticket sales, so Nelson, or Trident to be more specific, was forced to 'buy' Queen on to the tour. They paid £3,000 for the privilege of allowing Queen to support Mott The Hoople.

Ostensibly this money was to be used as a contribution to the on-the-road costs, but it was in practical terms a fee, and an exorbitant one too. It was precisely the kind of covert, but essential, assistance Queen required. It might technically have fallen within the broad definition of 'hype' but it was endemic within the industry and still is today.

Queen's rise to eminence coincided with a particularly dissolute period in the music business. The independent sector was still awaiting its genesis via punk rock, so in the absence of this healthy competition, a handful of major labels regularly resorted to dirty tricks to escalate sales. The charts, for example, were easy to manipulate. Most of the major labels knew the location of the few chart return shops and they employed teams to buy up stock the reps had often given to the retailer free of charge. Without the public even noticing, records went into the shop, out again, and, as a consequence, into the charts. Only then, would an artist's true popularity be measured.

Queen's first live performance outside the UK was in Frankfurt, Germany, on October 13, 1973, followed by a show the day afterwards at Le Blow Up Club in Luxembourg. EMI had organised several European radio and television interviews and many key people were invited to the shows. Radio Luxembourg planned to record the concert at Le Blow Up but there were technical problems and nothing was put down on to tape.

As a warm-up for the Mott The Hoople tour, Queen appeared at Imperial College on November 2. It was an undeniable coming of age celebration for Queen. The show was completely sold out, and many of their friends who arrived just a few minutes before they took the stage were unable to get in. They played three encores and it was plain that Queen, the ambitious but gauche 'pet band' of Imperial College, were no more; they were now tight, confident, and in their white satin shirts with pleated, billowing sleeves they were more stellar than anyone had noticed before.

Queen began their career as a bona fide touring rock group on November 12, 1973, when they opened for Mott The Hoople at Leeds Town Hall. It had been nearly a decade since all four members had first considered life in a pop group and started out in their respective teenage bands, The Opposition, The Reaction, 1984 and The Hectics. They had, individually and collectively, worked towards November 12, 1973, with incredible perseverance. There had been adversity and fiasco, providence and frolic, but, now, on the brink of real opportunity, their determination was fantastic.

The audiences up and down the UK, from The Central in Chatham, to the Apollo Theatre in Glasgow, adored Queen. Their set had been designed to elicit instant appeal. It was 45 minutes long and usually contained just six of their own songs, the final number given over to a rock'n'roll medley which they elongated or abridged depending on the crowd's response. Freddie Mercury, this unknown spidery figure in silk and Lycra, stalked the stage and dropped every ounce of himself into the performance. The band were tight, driving new life into songs they had been playing for years. The music press, understandably perhaps, considered it far too brazen and pantomime, but the word of mouth when Mott The Hoople fans were back at school, college or work the next day was that Queen were the business.

During the tour the band sometimes complained that they were not getting enough coverage in the press and Chris Poole, Tony Brainsby's assistant, had to placate them. "I had a good time with them but they were not an easy band," Poole stressed. "On the Mott The Hoople tour they were quite annoyed because they didn't get as much press as they figured they should have got. They may have been a support group, but they already had the mentality of stars."

By the final dates of the tour at Peterborough Town Hall and Liverpool's Top Rank Club, sales of Queen's début album had increased markedly. Eventually it reached number 24 and spent more than four months in the charts, no mean achievement for a new act at a time when competition was fierce.

Queen's appearance at the Top Rank in Liverpool was in support of 10cc and had been organised by Ken Testi, who had remained in close contact. Ken's own group, Great Day, were first on the bill and featured Freddie Mercury's first songwriting partner from Ibex, Mike Bersin. After the show, Ken Testi was travelling in the back of the van with Queen when they had to slow down as they passed the scene of a road accident near Huyton. "It was clearly a substantial accident, there was someone on a stretcher," said Ken Testi. "I made some remark to lighten the moment, with no disrespect intended. Brian and Roger were in the front. Roger was ashen, and they both reacted against the lightness of my remark. They were very sensitive people. Roger comes across with a lot of bravado but I know for a fact that there is a very sensitive side to Roger."

The New Year of 1974 started well for Queen when they were voted third 'best new band' by the readers of *Sounds*. They trailed the Scottish group Nazareth who had already scored three hits, and Blue, a trio whose self-titled début album had been warmly received, though it was to take them four years to register their one and only hit, 'Gonna Capture Your Heart'.

Queen's records had made only a negligible impact on Australasia, so two performances at Australia's celebrated Sunbury Music Festival in Melbourne in January 1974 were an ideal opportunity to infiltrate a growing market. However, only hours after receiving a series of injections necessary to travel to the sub-continent, Brian May's arm began to swell. He was in great pain and after a few days he was told he had gangrene in his arm, probably caused by a dirty needle.

Brian May recovered more quickly than expected and made the arduous journey with the band. Australia, with its known enmity to most things British, especially when it involved men dressed as women (as they doubtlessly saw Queen), was hardly ready for them, and Queen's needless ostentation served merely to hone the hostility. They hired gleaming white limousines to carry them from their hotel to the concert. Also, during the day of the concert, Queen's lighting crew had rowed with the local crew who couldn't understand why their services weren't required. The promoters placed Queen higher on the bill than several established Australian bands and this caused further animosity.

Queen took the stage - Freddie with an ear infection and Brian with a sore arm - only to face an unsympathetic compère: "Well, we've got another load of limey bastards here tonight. They're probably going to be useless, but let's give them something to think about." At that, the DJ took down his trousers and showed his bare backside to the crowd before shouting into the microphone that Queen were: 'Stuck up pommies.' During Queen's performance the lighting rig broke down, which their crew believed to be sabotage, and so, suitably disillusioned by Australia, Queen pulled the scheduled second performance on February 3 and flew back to the UK.

Their luck changed significantly when strenuous behind-the-scenes efforts led to a stroke of providence in February, 1974. EMI's head of promotion, Ronnie Fowler, had taken on Queen as a personal crusade. He had been smitten by the track 'Liar' but generally had an unconditional love of the band. The other new act he was charged with breaking was Steve Harley's Cockney Rebel but his commitment to Queen was such that Harley often grumbled about what he considered a bias towards Queen. Ronnie Fowler ran up expenses close to £20,000 on Queen alone. A large proportion of it went on meals and treats for key people as he undertook his almost evangelical mission.

On February 18 Ronnie Fowler's wheedling paid off handsomely when he received a phone call from Robin Nash, the producer of *Top Of The Pops*. He was told David Bowie was unable to appear on the show to perform 'Rebel Rebel' and a replacement was needed urgently. Robin Nash knew that Fowler would automatically suggest Queen, and they were indeed booked for the show two days later. The call to appear on the programme had come at a 'dead spot' for Queen when no single release was actually scheduled. EMI quickly activated its resources and in the space of a few hours a new Queen single was announced - 'Seven Seas Of Rhye'.

In the mid-Seventies *Top Of The Pops* was a tremendous, unrivalled shop window for the music industry. Its Thursday night spot was an institution and wonderfully timed to generate Saturday sales, the day when shops sold as many records as they did on all the other days of the week combined. Queen, through their début album and Mott The Hoople tour, had already established themselves as a laudable rock group, but *Top Of The Pops* was the ultimate vehicle for their commercial edge. They might well have broken without this early television exposure but it accelerated their acceptance.

EMI responded brilliantly to the opportunity and rush-released the single on February 23, just five days after the television appearance was confirmed. It entered the national charts two weeks later at number 45 and EMI, with its powerful network of pluggers and sales reps, was able to maintain the momentum and carry the single upwards. It eventually reached number 10 and spent more than two months in the charts. Royalties did not teem in for the band, and would not do so for some time yet, but Freddie felt secure enough to close his part-time stall at Kensington Market. Ronnie Fowler, who had done so much to propel the band, left EMI soon afterwards to join Elektra Records. "Roy Featherstone called me into his office when I finally left and threatened to sell my expense account to Steven Spielberg as a science fiction epic!" he said.

The success of 'Seven Seas Of Rhye' was fortuitously timed since it came on the eve of Queen's first headlining tour. They rehearsed for the planned twenty-three-date tour at Ealing film studios and decided to close their set for the first time without resorting to rock'n'roll numbers like 'Jailhouse Rock' and 'Shake Rattle And Roll'. In itself it was only a minor amendment but it showed a growing confidence in their own material. Freddie insisted, though, that 'Big Spender' remained in their canon and the number, effectively included for light relief, stayed for a good number of years.

Queen were writing new songs at a rapid pace, still tripping over themselves in terms of their recorded and live work. They had completed 'Queen II' in the space of a month at the end of the summer of 1973, yet in rehearsal they were running through songs like 'Now I'm Here', 'Killer Queen', 'Bring Back That Leroy Brown' and 'In The Lap Of The Gods', tracks which would not be released until the 'Sheer Heart Attack' album at the end of 1974.

Their first headlining tour began inauspiciously at the Winter Gardens, Blackpool, on March 1, when the truck carrying Queen's lighting rig broke down some distance from the venue. The concert ran late and the next night, at Friar's in Aylesbury, Queen had to cut short their set when Brian May was in too much pain from his arm to continue.

Queen were joined the next night at the Plymouth Guild Hall by the support group, Nutz, who were to play with them through the rest of the tour. The two bands had been effectively married together by John Anthony. The producer had been called in to produce Nutz's début album for A&M Records after earlier attempts to lay their soft rock on to tape had been a calamity. "John Anthony came along and rescued the first album for us," said Dave Lloyd, the singer with Nutz. "John went for thick sounding guitars and layered harmonies. I think he'd learned a little bit from Brian May."

The members of Nutz - Dave Lloyd (vocals/guitar), Mick Devenport (lead guitar), Keith Mulholland (bass) and John Mylett (drums) - had first been introduced to Queen at their rehearsal base in Ealing. "These guys came out in nail varnish and fur coats and we thought how different they were from us," said Dave Lloyd. "They seemed very sensitive and had a kind of grand plan and we were four crazy scousers."

The two groups complemented each other well and Nutz soon developed a high regard for Queen. "They were great, really friendly guys," said Dave Lloyd. "They had no airs and graces. Freddie was always liable to fly off the handle if things weren't going to plan. We played The Rainbow and Freddie stormed off to the band's camper van. The rest of them carried on with the sound check and Brian shouted into the microphone, 'Come back Freddie, you old tart.' Freddie was sometimes very nervous about going on stage. He was sick with nerves on the first night."

Queen took a benevolent attitude towards their support band and though they were only really novices themselves, they were keen to help. Freddie heard that Nutz were staying in low-grade guest houses and berated their management for being miserly; Nutz were usually invited back to Queen's hotel after the shows. "They did not take any nasty liberties and they were quite good about the whole thing of us being their support band," said Dave Lloyd. "They tried to get us a longer soundcheck and things like that." Freddie Mercury, though he has often been portrayed as a prima donna, had a spirited view to performance, even in adversity, as Dave Lloyd discovered. "We were due to play at Aberystwyth University and it was one of those formal balls. They had a steel band in one room and it didn't feel like a proper concert at all. I remember telling Freddie all this in the hotel and he just said, 'Oh David, you can be such a cunt, we'll do well tonight'."

The tour was another resounding success for Queen, but it featured the usual assortment of drama: the lighting crew walked out in Glasgow over internal arguments; two people were stabbed in a brawl at Stirling; a power cut interrupted the performance at London's Rainbow Theatre; Dave Lloyd streaked across the stage in Birmingham during Queen's set; thieves raided Queen's van in Manchester; the audience sang 'God Save The Queen' spontaneously at Plymouth - all standard rock 'n' roll fare.

'Queen II' was delayed when the band spotted a spelling mistake on the sleeve. It meant that its release on March 8, 1974, came when the tour to promote the record was already under way. The artwork for the sleeve had been devised by photographer Mick Rock. He was given a vague brief; it would be a gatefold sleeve in black and white, otherwise it was an open canvas. Rock had recently befriended a collector of Hollywood stills called John Kobal who had given him copies of his treasured prints. "Among them was one I had never seen before of Marlene Dietrich from the film Shanghai Express," said Rock. "Her arms were folded and she was wearing black against a black background, and it was exquisitely lit. Her tilted head and hands seemed to be floating. I saw the connection immediately. It was one of those visceral, instinctive things. Very strong. Very clear. Glamorous, mysterious and classic. I would transpose it into a four-headed monster. They had to go for it. So I went to Freddie. He saw it too. He understood. He loved it immediately. And he sold the rest of the band on it. 'I shall be Marlene,' he laughed."

The image conceived by Mick Rock was to become indelibly linked with the band and had a momentous impact as a 'branding' of the group – perhaps rivalled only by Freddie Mercury's Live Aid persona. Surprisingly, apart from Freddie, the other band members were initially sceptical about the portrait. "There was some concern that the photos might be almost too strong, pretentious even, to some eyes," said Rock. "And they had a point. Fortunately Freddie was never scared of pretension. He loved to quote Oscar Wilde. So he wore the others down and the right decision was made."

The critical response to 'Queen II' was again varied. *Sounds* said it 'captured them in their finest hours' while *Record Mirror* claimed Queen were the 'dregs of glam rock.' The *Record Mirror* review was written by Chris Poole, Tony Brainsby's former assistant who had moved into journalism. Queen considered Poole's article an act of betrayal and their response was decisive. "I didn't like the album, slagged it off, and they never forgave me," said Chris Poole. "We didn't talk for eight years and it has only been in the last six years that they have spoken to me." While Poole's review lacked discretion, it hardly merited Queen's zealous retort, and again revealed their sometimes rather austere, unforgiving demeanour.

Brian May considered 'Queen II' the first real testament to Queen's distinctive sound. "Led Zeppelin and The Who are probably in there somewhere because they were among our favourite groups, but what we were trying to do different from either of those groups was this sort of layered sound," said Brian May. "To me, 'Queen II' was the sort of emotional music we'd always wanted to be able to play, although we couldn't play most of it on stage because it was too complicated. We were trying to push studio techniques to a new limit for rock groups - it was fulfilling all our dreams because we didn't have much opportunity for that on the first album. It went through our minds to call the album, 'Over The Top'."

Despite its profuse arrangements and erratic metre, 'Queen II' sold much better than the début album and reached number 5, spending most of the rest of the year in the chart. By September 1974 it had sold more than 100,000 copies in the UK, earning the band a silver disc which they marked with a party at London's Café Royal. It was a grandiosely ambitious record, a Rubik's cube for the ears, but it was a record Queen needed to make, if only to help them expunge their over-complex, progressive leanings. They had demonstrated their aesthetic musicianship and were now free to hone it down to indispensable pop singles.

Elektra had done some excellent ground work in the United States without the band having played there or undertaken any real promotion. The début album had made number 83 and 'Queen II' just shaded into the Top Fifty - two extremely encouraging showings for a non-American band with a relatively low profile. It was evident that Queen had a core of support in the US, so the offer to support Mott The Hoople there in the spring of 1974 was relished.

After a show in Louisiana, their sixth of the tour, Brian May complained of feeling unwell. He played on for three more weeks but after Queen's sixth consecutive performance supporting Mott at New York's Uris Theater, he collapsed and was diagnosed as having hepatitis. Queen pulled out of the tour, their place taken by Kansas, who were about to release their début album, 'Masque'.

Brian May spent most of the summer of 1974 recovering while the rest of the band began recording their third album, 'Sheer Heart Attack', at Rockfield Studios in Wales. He visited intermittently to record his guitar parts but in August he was again rushed to hospital, this time suffering a duodenal ulcer. The second illness meant that a tour of the US scheduled for the autumn had to be scrapped. From his sick bed Brian May wrote lyrics and strummed his guitar when he could, and fully completed a song which was later a hit, 'Now I'm Here'. The sessions for 'Sheer Heart Attack' were finished at Trident and the band were appreciative of Roy Thomas-Baker's ability to lay Brian May's guitar parts and vocal harmonies on to the half-finished tracks.

The public's first taste of Queen's new material came on October 11, 1974, with the release of the double A-sided single 'Killer Queen'/'Flick Of The Wrist'. It was the most important record of the band's career, establishing them as a genuine pop force. Hitherto, the issue had been somewhat fudged. They were perceived as a rock group, but missed the phlegmatic intensity of, say, Black Sabbath or Deep Purple. Queen, like all great groups, were fundamentally original and the melodic, debonair 'Killer Queen' was the counter-balance to the laboured complexity of tracks like 'Ogre Battle' or 'The Fairy Feller's Masterstroke'. "People are used to hard rock, energy music from Queen, yet this single, you almost expect Noël Coward to sing it," explained Freddie Mercury. "It's one of those bowler hat, black suspender belt numbers – not that Noël Coward would wear that."

The single entered the chart at number 5 before spending two weeks at number 2 where it was held off the top spot by David Essex's 'Gonna Make You A Star'. The tour to promote the single and forthcoming album was designed on a lavish scale, the band adding a new lighting rig and various pyrotechnic effects to the stage show. Queen were supported by Hustler, another group who, like Nutz before them, were signed to A&M but failed to record a hit.

The tour, with tickets priced at £1.30 began at the Palace Theatre, Manchester. The set was longer than ever before, featuring almost twenty songs, and it ended with a version of the National Anthem recorded beforehand by the band. After the second concert, at Leeds University, Roger Taylor had to be taken to hospital with a foot injury. His stage monitor had failed and afterwards he had thrown a temper tantrum and kicked the dressing-room wall.

'Sheer Heart Attack' was released on November 8 and reached number 2 in the charts. The reviews, even in previously hostile quarters like the *NME*, were favourable. 'A feast. No duffers,' summarised its reviewer. Paradoxically, Brian May's illness might well have focused the writing and recording of the album, sparing it the indulgences of the previous two. Brian May appeared to acknowledge the fact in a magazine interview: "We weren't going for a hit, because we always thought of ourselves as an albums group, but we did think that perhaps we'd dished up a bit too much for people to swallow on 'Queen II'."

The UK tour closed at the Rainbow Theatre in London. Tickets sold out in just two days so another date was added and they played two consecutive nights on November 19 and 20. The second performance was filmed and later edited down to a 30-minute film. It was later screened in British cinemas as a support film to Led Zeppelin's *The Song Remains The Same*.

Queen's hectic schedule continued with their first European tour which began just three days after the performance at the Rainbow Theatre. Opening in Gothenburg, they played ten shows in six countries before finishing on December 10 in Barcelona. All the shows were completely sold out and in Barcelona 6,000 tickets had been sold in one day.

John Deacon returned to Oadby to spend the Christmas of 1974 with his friends and family. 'Killer Queen' had slipped out of the charts and John's friend, Dave Williams, barely noticed when the intro broke forth from a juke-box in a pub where they were drinking a few days before Christmas. "John said something like, 'Oh no, here we go' and I wondered what he meant," Dave recalls. "I didn't think anyone really knew who he was or had recognised him, but right away people started coming over asking for autographs. He tried to keep his head down but he had to sign a few."

On another occasion John Deacon collected his old friend from The Opposition, Nigel Bullen, in a Jensen Healey sports car and they drove deep into the countryside purposely to avoid John being recognised. They arrived at The

Wheel and Compass pub in Weston-by-Welland near to Market Harborough. Nigel Bullen noticed that his friend no longer drank beer and had ordered gin and tonics; he also introduced Nigel to Chablis ("I remember it cost about a fiver which was a lot those days."). Inevitably, John Deacon was spotted and was soon asked for his autograph. Nigel Bullen had expected as much since John was wearing a Queen tour jacket. "He hated being recognised, he was really embarrassed about it," he said. "Once we were out and he refused to sign any autographs. I don't remember what I thought about that. I think Queen might have had a policy at the time of not doing them."

Of the gang left behind in Oadby, Nigel Bullen was undoubtedly the closest to John Deacon, and few were surprised when John asked him to be the Best Man at his wedding on January 18, 1975. "I was absolutely bricking it, knowing I'd have to do my speech in front of all those performers and his management people," he said.

John Deacon had been dating Veronica Tetzlaff since his early days at university. Sheffield-born of Polish ancestry, Veronica had studied at the Maria Assumpta Teacher Training College before starting work as a nanny. Nigel Bullen's wife, Ruth, got to know her quite well through their husbands' friendship. "She's a very normal, very quiet devout Catholic," she said. "She didn't wear any make-up and wore fairly plain clothes; she wasn't into the glamorous life at all. She is a lovely person, completely unpretentious. I've got the impression down the years that their children are the most important things to her."

Ruth Bullen recalls Veronica's response when, early in their marriage, John Deacon bought her a new Mini car. "She was thrilled to bits with it. A lot would have bought something top of the range, but she did not come from money and was just happy to have a car. It took her a few years to realise she could have practically anything she wanted. It was ages before she got a nanny to help her with the kids."

Nigel Bullen travelled to London on the day before the wedding for a briefing from John Deacon. He lived in a flat close to Parsons Green Tube station in Fulham and their conversation was frequently interrupted by the tremor of Tube trains passing close by. They discussed the wedding arrangements over a bottle of Southern Comfort after a meal at a local restaurant.

The wedding took place at a Carmelite church in Kensington Church Street. Veronica's family were members of this order of Catholicism, named after Mount Carmel in Palestine, and dedicated to a strictly orthodox application of the faith. Carmelite nuns, once inducted, had, until very recently, to maintain a vow of complete silence.

It was a long wedding service addressed by a friar, but the proceedings had been lightened beforehand by the arrival of Freddie Mercury. Nigel Bullen: "The doors burst open at the back of the church and all we could see was this silhouette of a figure with a girl on each arm, I think one of them was Mary Austin. At first I thought it was the bride, but then I realised it was Freddie! He was wearing a feather boa and everyone in the room turned to look. It was some entrance."

The reception was to be held at Veronica's flat in Hammersmith and Nigel, doing his utmost in torrid circumstances, was trying to get too many people into not enough cars. He suddenly hit upon an idea. "We only had a couple of cars and it was my job to make sure everyone got to the reception," says Bullen. "Freddie was in this stretch limo, his own car I think, with these two girls. I stuck my head through the window and said, 'Room for a few more?' We crammed all these people in. He didn't say anything, but his face was a picture and it was really comical. His feather boa must have got well crushed."

Nigel Bullen remained fairly close to John Deacon in the mid-Seventies, often staying with him and Veronica, enjoying the dashes of affluence, like being driven to Queen's London shows in a chauffeur driven Jaguar. Eventually, the two friends drifted apart. Nigel and Ruth Bullen watched impotently as a gauze was placed over John Deacon, fame spiriting him away like an apparition. Nigel would call on him whenever he was in London but John was never around. He was away, touring, or 'cooking up business' as Veronica would tell them. And when they were infrequently reunited it was compromised, a shade awkward, no longer the same as before; a few stolen moments backstage, John's mind apparently on a thousand other things. The Bullens did not know how to respond, there was no formal training in maintaining a friendship altered by fame. If they chased him to ground they felt like sycophants, anxious to touch the cloth, gluttons for glamour, but if they ignored him they wondered whether John felt shunned, his past deserting him.

Ruth Bullen used to sometimes see John Deacon's mother, Molly Deacon, in Oadby and she told her that she was concerned about her son. "I think she used to worry about him a lot," she said. "She said all the pressure used to make him a bit ill. Veronica said when he came back off a tour he couldn't revert to being a normal person, playing with the kids, taking them to the park and things. She said it was non-stop, he just couldn't stop. I don't suppose you can live the life he has without paying a price."

Finally, on Queen's UK tour of 1985, Nigel Bullen accepted that the chasm between his own life and John Deacon's was too vast to span. He attended the massively popular shows in Leeds, Birmingham and London and was astounded by how the behemoth of stardom now held his former school friend. "There was so much security, it was unbelievable," said Bullen. "Even if you knew him, like his mum for example, she still had to go through all the security channels. I saw her waiting to be let backstage into certain places. Once we were in with him it was fine, we had a drink and a chat. He'd click his fingers and ask what we wanted and someone would get it for us. There were all these hangers-on, just making sure he was OK. It was very unnatural. It was such a lot of organisation just to make sure that four men were kept happy all of the time. They were there for his every whim. He had changed from how I remembered him. He had lost some of that enthusiasm of the early Seventies, and had an attitude of, 'Well, we've made it now.' I don't think you could possibly go through all that without changing though."

After sampling the opulence of backstage Queen in 1985, Nigel Bullen inevitably found it an anti-climax to return to everyday life at his job in the textile industry. He was twice made redundant in the Eighties and now runs his own small textile company with Ruth on a draughty industrial estate just a few miles from Oadby. The Christmas cards from the Bullens to the Deacons and vice versa no longer pass in the post in December and the two friends have not met for nearly a decade. Nigel is nonchalant, he's lost touch with others from his past, life goes on. As he looks out from under the sign 'N. Bullen Textiles', he's convinced that one of the other units, on the other side of the car park and the wire perimeter fence, could very well have been: 'J. Deacon Electronics'.

A Silhouette
Of A Man

Chapter XII

Posters on bedroom walls, articles in newspapers, venues sold out, people constantly seeking an autograph, songs on the radio - evidence of Queen's success was everywhere by the beginning of 1975. Naturally, people assumed Queen's fame was matched by their prosperity. It was bizarre, therefore, that after selling out venues holding nearly 3,000 people they should return to their modest rented flats and houses. Brian May lived in a dreary room in a house in South Kensington, and the only access to it was through a steamy downstairs boiler room. Freddie's flat was damp with fungus on the ceiling and John Deacon was desperate for money to put down as a deposit on a new house for himself and Veronica.

They petitioned Trident and Norman Sheffield agreed to treble their weekly allowance to £60 per band member. It was far in excess of the average weekly wage in 1975, but in comparison to the cash coming in via concerts, record sales and publishing royalties it was a pittance. Queen tried to persuade Trident to provide 'gifts' as an alternative to cash sums, but Roger Taylor's request for a car and Freddie Mercury's for a piano went unheeded.

In its allegedly miserly treatment of Queen, it is easy to perceive Trident as unscrupulous, but the business of finance in the music industry is inordinately complex. Basically, all the money invested by Trident in Queen was recoverable before any profits would be shared out. This meant Queen had to 'pay back' Trident for considerable expenses like the recording costs of the first album; wages for retainers like Jack Nelson and Tony Brainsby; and sundries like hotel bills on tour, road crew wages and the fee to support Mott The Hoople. From the very beginning Queen had an obsession with professionalism, the best money could buy, and it was usually Trident that paid the high price for this fervent commitment. For example, 'Sheer Heart Attack', although funded by EMI and not Trident, cost an estimated £30,000 to record, an immense amount at the time.

Obviously, when the hit singles arrived, Queen were impatient to receive some of the funds they were generating. It was a natural instinct, an assumption fuelled by their friends' incredulity when they were told of the paltry wage they were receiving. It didn't seem right, but, in the accounting system used by the music business, it rarely did. Similarly, anyone examining the situation before the hit singles, when Trident was thousands in arrears to a group who were demanding nothing but the best, would have sympathised with the company.

The situation was compounded by the multiplicity of agreements which Queen had signed with Trident. This meant that unlike other artists who could, for example, earn royalties from record sales or song publishing while they resolved a management dispute, practically all of Queen's income, or lack of it, came via Trident. There was a myriad of technical quarrels and contradictions between Queen and Trident, and indeed between Jack Nelson, Queen and Trident. The contract had been too ambitious from the beginning, far too cloying, but it was only - as in all contracts - when it was tested that the deficiencies came to the surface. At one point, while Queen were arguing earnestly that John Deacon should receive £4,000 to enable him to buy a house for himself and pregnant wife, Trident revealed that Queen actually owed £190,000 to the company.

In retrospect, Trident should have opted to appease the band and pay them more money, if only to protect its investment for a longer period. It refused to budge beyond its offer of £60 per week, however, and so, in December 1974, Queen employed the services of a music business lawyer, Jim Beach, to help extricate themselves from the Trident contract.

Despite the contractual problems, Queen travelled to the United States at the end of January, 1975, to start a lengthy tour that would take in 38 shows. Organised by the well-known British concert promoter, Mel Bush, the tour began in Columbus, Ohio on February 5. Fourteen shows later, Freddie was complaining of severe throat pains and a specialist at Philadelphia University Hospital diagnosed nodes and advised him not to sing for three months. He defied the doctor and sang that very night. Another specialist advised Freddie that a rest of a week or two would allow his throat to recover, so Queen restarted the tour on March 5 in Wisconsin.

Like Queen, Jack Nelson had his own brooding altercation with Trident. It would appear that Trident was not deducting a percentage from Queen's royalty account to direct specifically into a management ledger. This meant Nelson was on a quasi-wage rather than a profit-linked share of the money accrued by Queen. As he had devoted the best part of two years to Queen's cause, it was understandable that he would feel disappointed. In the music business, unlike almost any other, its players expect to earn money in perpetuity for their efforts, not fixed sums (even extraordinarily high ones) for a limited period. Usually managers, A&R staff, producers and even sundry courtiers agree on 'points' - a percentage drawn from royalties that often last throughout a group or record's lifetime. In July 1974, Jack Nelson left the employ of Trident, and consequently, Queen.

Queen were aware that their records had been well received in Japan, but nothing could have prepared them for the response they received when they landed in Tokyo in April 1975. There were 3,000 exuberant fans waving banners, blowing kisses, clicking away with pocket cameras, and the bewildered looks on Queen's faces revealed the depth of their surprise. Japan had taken to Queen on an unparalleled scale. In the opinion of its youth, Queen were bona fide pin-ups. "Suddenly we were stars," said Brian May. "We'd had some success in England and America, but we hadn't had adulation and been adored, and suddenly, in Japan, we were pop stars in the same way as The Beatles and The Bay City Rollers, with people screaming at us, which was a big novelty, and we loved it and had a great time." It is easy to plot an affinity between Queen's image and the traditional clothing work by geishas, but this is to overlook the capacity of the Japanese to embrace the new with ingenuous passion.

Queen's commitment and devotion to their Japanese fans was absolute. Unlike many of their contemporaries they did not pay lip service to the country simply because it was on the other side of the world. Their first Japanese tour embraced several major cities including Tokyo, Nagoya, Kobe, Fukuoka, Okayama, Shizuoka and Yokohama. Even on this first tour, Japanese film crews, recognising the significance of the band, were making documentaries and some of the venues, like the famous Budokan Hall in Tokyo, held up to 10,000 fans - more than three times as many as Queen's typical UK venue. Japan, like the US, had phenomenal spending power, and this fact had not escaped Queen, EMI or Trident. Japan and the US together were the two most important 'territories' in the world and Queen's early and determined incursion on this lucrative market was a masterful strategy. It ensured that their income, and marvellous future wealth, was bedded in the most fertile soil on earth.

Time away from Queen was scarce, but early in 1975 Freddie Mercury stole a couple of weeks to work with an aspiring singer/songwriter called Ed Howell. Along with his friend, David Minns, who was managing Howell, Freddie attended a show at the Thursday Club in Kensington where Howell was previewing material from his début album, the prosaically titled (and deliberately misspelled) 'Eddie Howell's Gramaphone Record'. Signed to Warners as a solo performer, Howell had already eked out a modest reputation as a staff writer for Chrysalis Publishing.

The Thursday Club show was beset with problems; the power failed after just twenty minutes and the rest of the set had to be performed acoustically. David Minns, with support from Warners' charismatic publicity officer, Moira Bellas, had cajoled a good number of celebrities to come to the event and Phil Collins joined Ed on stage to play congas. Freddie also considered taking the stage but respectfully held back, not wishing to possibly eclipse Ed.

After the performance Ed Howell joined David Minns and Freddie who were sharing a table with the DJ Kenny Everett and his wife, Lee Everett. They moved on together to the White Elephant nightclub on the banks of the River Thames. Freddie reassured Ed that it had been a successful show. "I was obviously a bit nervous about meeting him, but I could tell he was a very generous bloke, generous in spirit," said Ed Howell.

"He was really up about everything and made a bit of a fuss. He was fairly flamboyant in his dress and demeanour but there was a heart beating in there."

Freddie was particularly captivated by Ed Howell's song, 'The Man From Manhattan'. The lyrics had been inspired by the Mario Puzo book, *The Godfather Papers*, and were written on Howell's return from a holiday in New York. He was intrigued at the time by the double moral standards of the Mafia and envisaged the song as pop sleaze, with haunting trombones and a muse not dissimilar to The Kinks' 'Dead End Street'. Freddie asked for a demo tape of the track and a few days afterwards a limousine called at Ed Howell's flat to take him to Freddie's house in Holland Park.

Ed Howell soon realised that his own design for 'The Man From Manhattan' was set for burial under Freddie's avalanche of ideas. "It was difficult for me to maintain the original idea," he said. "I have worked with quite a few people since but none of them quite like Freddie. He was like a kid in a toy shop. He worked his way meticulously through every note of the song. I vividly remember him sitting at this huge Yamaha grand piano in his flat. He was so keen to work that he had a tape recorder with him when he picked me up in the limo and he would be singing ideas into it."

Word reached Warners, and its staff were understandably delighted to have a fairly established star produce one of their embryonic artists. Budgets had previously been tight (Ed had released three singles which had not charted in the UK) but money was suddenly made available as Warners presumed Freddie's sanction would stimulate Ed Howell's career. For his part, Freddie was 'just another muso' when around Ed: "He would turn up in the limo and dressed as if he was going on stage, dressed to kill I suppose, but that was the way he was, full on. But when we were all sat around the piano in the studio he did his utmost to create an air of equality."

At Freddie's request, the recordings took place at Sarm East Studios in Brick Lane, Whitechapel. Two renowned session musicians were hired as a rhythm section, Barry de Souza on drums and Jerome Rimson on bass. Ed Howell played acoustic guitar, Freddie the piano and backing vocals, and Brian May the lead guitar parts. Ed Howell had previously produced his own material in a strictly monitored environment and was quietly astounded by the new modus operandi. Freddie insisted that no one from Warners should visit the studio and expense was no consideration. He would adjourn sessions if he felt the mood was not right and the team, tea boys and tape operators included, would visit one of the celebrated curry houses along the nearby Brick Lane. The studio bill, which was £60 per hour at peak time, was even allowed to run up while Freddie sent someone out to find a bell to be sounded at the very end of the song. The bell arrived late and the party was by then ensconced in another Indian restaurant. The search for the bell and the 'dead' hours it created in studio time had cost Warners nearly £400.

Inevitably, Ed Howell 'lost' the song as his own, but remained philosophical. "I had this really concrete idea, the trombones and everything, but it became this Queen thing," he said. "It was difficult to maintain my identity. It did not go the way I envisaged but Freddie stretched me and it was an important part of my musical development. He was such a professional, so dedicated to what he was doing." During recordings, with Freddie lost in the vibes, he often quipped to Ed: "If this isn't a hit we'll sue someone."

The song had started to pick up regular radio airplay when the Musicians' Union suddenly intervened. It had been informed that Jerome Rimson, an American, was neither a member of the union nor in possession of a work permit. During the Seventies the union was highly proprietorial, sometimes its zealousness actually impeded a musician's career. Television appearances on influential programmes like *Top Of The Pops* were lined up but they had to be pulled. Ed Howell was left with a single that reached the Top 40 throughout the rest of Europe but failed to chart in his home country. Freddie, to his credit, had freely allowed his name to be associated with the project (indeed, he was very proud of the record), but he was out of touch - enmeshed once more in Queen business - as the record slipped quietly from the public's grasp. Ed Howell was eventually released from his contract with Warners but continued writing songs for other performers, including Frida Lyngstad Fredriksson from Abba and Samantha Fox. In 1995 he secured the rights to 'The Man From Manhattan' and released it again on his own label, Bud Records.

During the summer of 1975 Queen properly addressed the dispute with Trident, though it was to prove very expensive. In aggregate terms, the corollary of the negotiations was that Queen had to pay Trident severance pay of £100,000 (which was covered by an advance from EMI Publishing) and a one per cent royalty on their forthcoming six albums. Trident, for its part, agreed to relinquish its claim on the band's management, production and sub-publishing.

Although management heavyweights Don Arden and Peter Grant had shown lukewarm interest, Queen eventually replaced Jack Nelson with John Reid, the Scot who had masterminded Elton John's remarkable rise to fame. Jim Beach was still working industriously on the band's behalf and was to remain by their side permanently, dealing with the abundance of financial affairs.

In the midst of this management discord, Freddie worked on a song which was to become a bench mark in the history of rock. The potential for an idiosyncratic and classic song had been there almost from the beginning, indeed many of the elements fully realised on 'Bohemian Rhapsody' were present in skeletal form on 'Queen'. Before he started on the song, Freddie Mercury had a distinct idea of how it would be arranged. "It didn't just come out of thin air," said Freddie. "I did a bit of research, although it was tongue-in-cheek and a mock opera. Why not? I certainly wasn't saying I was an opera fanatic and I knew everything about it."

It was nearly six minutes long and Freddie faced great pressure to edit it down, especially from John Reid, but he steadfastly refused. He was unsure, however, whether it would be a commercial hit and sought the advice of his good friend, Kenny Everett, who assured him it would be 'number one for centuries'. "He was very unsure about this piece of genius," said Everett. "It was very odd when you look back on it, because it was so great. It was like Mozart saying, 'I don't know if my clarinet concerto is going to take off'. It's silly really. I mean, it's got number one written all over it from the first note."

Ken Testi visited Queen during the recording of 'Bohemian Rhapsody' and hung out with them for a few days. He visited the studio with Roger Taylor to listen to how the song was developing. "They were doing Brian's overdubs at the time," Testi recalls. "I was unaccustomed to overdubbing and this backwards and forwards stuff. It was very hard for me to get a handle on it, it was impossible to understand. At the end they played the whole track through to me and I still couldn't get my head around it. I asked Freddie would anyone play it and he said, 'Of course they'll play it, my dear. It's going to be fucking huge'."

Delighted to meet up with his old friends again, Ken Testi detected an aura of exhilaration within the group, probably brought about by their disentanglement from the Trident contract. "I especially noticed that Mary and Freddie were lovely together," Ken said. "She was a lovely woman and always fussing over Freddie. He would ring her from wherever he was and ask her to send over some cotton socks post haste, that kind of thing. They both seemed to have a shared pleasure in other people's company, they took pleasure in entertaining. They were always able to make an occasion out of humble ingredients. They lived in this first floor bedsit with a tiny kitchenette but had managed to get these really nice plates with a nice design and they couldn't wait to have people around."

John Deacon was the newcomer to Queen, at least as far as Ken Testi was concerned, and Ken was interested to know how he was considered by the others. "He was clearly quieter than them, and I asked them what they thought of him," Ken recalls. "I thought that they might be finding him tough-going, but they had warmed to him very quickly. They were sure he'd stay the course. They said he was a good chap and just what they needed."

On a drinking session in Putney, Ken Testi discovered that Roger Taylor had not changed his irregular ways. "It was a real beer and skittles pub," Ken recalls. "Roger ordered a Mackeson and I said, 'What did you want to order one of them for?' He said, 'Well, no one else is drinking it'. Roger always wanted to be different than everyone else. He would never wear jeans because of that. He was always the one who was going to be the most susceptible to stardom and I'm glad he got what he wanted. I think it mattered most to him."

Ken Testi returned to Liverpool and submerged himself once more in the music scene. He managed the influential Deaf School which featured Clive Langer, who went on to become a respected producer, rising to prominence chiefly through his work with the band Madness. Ken was also a major figure behind Eric's, the Liverpool club which played host to the burgeoning new wave scene.

Unavoidably, Testi's meetings with Queen became infrequent, though the band (minus Freddie) visited a jazz club he was running, during a night off on their 1977 tour. "I met up the next day with Brian May and we had tea and biscuits at the Adelphi Hotel," Testi remembers. "We went to the Pier Head and sat together on top of a building by a landing stage. It was just me and Brian with his minder walking up and down behind us. I don't think he really needed the minder, we were miles away from any one. We both had a good heart to heart, it was absolutely lovely. It was rare to find Brian actually seeming happy. He is a gentle soul given to deep thought. I don't think he's capable of a flippant answer, but that's not to say he's not humourous." As the two friends walked back towards the waiting vehicle, Ken Testi was overtaken by memories. An image of Queen on stage came to mind, Freddie in full swing, the audience screaming their adoration. He then remembered Freddie sitting quietly in his Liverpool home, patiently teaching his youngest daughter how to play draughts.

'Bohemian Rhapsody' took three weeks to record and in places featured 180 vocal over dubs. It was recorded in separate sections, held together merely by a drum click to keep it in time. Much of the middle section was 'busked' with Freddie returning to the studio constantly to add extra vocals.

To accompany the single, Queen decided to shoot a promotional film at Elstree Film Studios. In just four hours on November 10, 1975, and at a cost of £4,500, they created the first successful promotional video, and also one of the most memorable. Directed by Bruce Gowers, it borrowed heavily from the cover image created originally by Mick Rock for 'Queen II' but the otherwise eerie, shadowy film had much of its own striking imagery. The degree to which it later planted itself on the nation's psyche was remarkable.

The single was a taster of the band's forthcoming album, 'A Night At The Opera' and the UK tour to promote both records began at the Liverpool Empire on November 14. During the first part of the tour 'Bohemian Rhapsody' made a fairly unspectacular ascent of the charts, almost as if it was taking the public time to absorb, comprehend, and, finally, enjoy it. It entered the chart at number 47, rose to seventeen, nine, and then, on November 25, while Queen were in a hotel preparing to appear at the Gaumont in Southampton, they learned they had scored their first ever number 1.

Queen, and the four people within the group, had accomplished their dream. The journies which began in a tiny Leicestershire village, in the rich green fields of Cornwall, on the black pitch streets of London's suburbia, and on the plains of Poona, were now complete. Their passage had taught them much about human nature; greed and generosity, opportunism and perseverance. They had in a few years touched upon emotions and experiences others would take a lifetime to encounter. Simultaneously, their own personalities had been amended in response to this imaginary world they had created within the real world.

The proxy people - publicists, advisors, spokesmen, lackeys - could each relate the authorised, burnished view of the musicians who comprised Queen, but their comments were always at the bequest of the mothership. Perhaps the most sincere commentary of the Queen of December 1975 - number 1 in the charts, their faces looking out from every television, concert halls packed to screaming pitch - would come from an outsider hidden in the shadows, the obligatory enormous bunch of keys hanging from his belt.

In on-the-road terms, Trevor Cooper was in the lowest caste of all. A roadie for the support group, Mr Big, he was in the metaphorical cheap seats, but the vantage point was ideal for a crystalline view of Queen. "They really were good guys," he says without hesitation. "They demanded perfection and Freddie would sometimes throw tantrums but it was because he always wanted things to be right. You could tell Freddie was gay by his effeminate gestures but he could swear like the best of them. He'd be 'fuck this' and 'fuck that' and the next minute he was calling everyone 'darling' and having a laugh." There was confirmation of Queen's 'good guys' status – they let Mr Big borrow their equipment; Brian May paid them the respect of watching them almost every night; no one was 'chewed off' in front of anyone else; and Roger Taylor even played football with a handful of roadies using a cabbage at a hotel in Bristol.

In Manchester, at a show at the city's Free Trade Hall, Trevor Cooper witnessed Freddie's poise and strength of personality. "I saw him literally shrink this six foot bloke down to an inch," he recalls. "Queen had just taken the stage and this bloke shouted to Freddie, 'You fucking poof', or something like that. Freddie demanded that the crew turn the spotlight on the crowd and find this fella. He then said to him, 'Say that again, darling' and the bloke didn't know what to do. Everyone was laughing. He just had this ability to cream an audience, milk it. If he'd have said take your clothes off, they would have done. He was a showman, one of only very few in the world."

The tour crew all noted John Harris' remarkable dedication to Queen. He had remained the 'fifth' member of Queen through all the business machinations and his position at the sound desk was as indisputable as Freddie's at the front of the stage. "That bloke ate, drank and slept Queen," said Cooper. "It was all he thought about, all he cared about. He didn't seem to have any other life. He taped every single show and when we were on the tour bus the next day he would be listening to it through his headphones, he was that keen to get it spot-on night after night. If things were going wrong, effects not working or an instrument not sounding right, I think John used to take it too much to heart. He seemed to think it was his job to do something about that kind of thing but it wasn't his fault. The band didn't give him a hard time, but it was as if nothing else mattered in his life."

Girls were constantly pestering the group, and the roadies shamelessly exploited the situation. They were generally promised that in order to meet the group, they first had to have sex with them. Trevor Cooper had full sex with eighteen girls during the tour, while a lighting roadie had twenty-four. "And they weren't dogs either," insists the rapacious Cooper. "Nowadays we would have been dead. Freddie was just unlucky. Queen seemed to be really clean living then, they always seemed to be around their girlfriends. There was no sordid stuff. I only read about Freddie in Hamburg and all that stuff after he died. When I knew him he wasn't anything like that. Maybe he was trying to get to where he wanted to be and once he got there he changed."

'Bohemian Rhapsody' spent nine weeks at number 1 and had sold more than one million copies in the UK by the end of January 1976. 'A Night At The Opera' also reached number 1 and within two months had sold 500,000 copies. Only Abba, whose 'Mama Mia' superseded 'Bohemian Rhapsody' at the top of the charts, sold more albums than Queen during 1976. The Swedish group lasted until 1983 when, caught hopelessly out of time, the hits dried up and the petty arguments ran to spleen. Queen? They stayed together, grew older, argued occasionally, laughed occasionally, changed with the times, had more hit records, enraptured the world at Live Aid, and then, on November 24, 1991, a loathsome disease caused the death of their singer and main songwriter - someone who had never been just a silhouette of a man.

Epilogue

Queen

It's one of those dead mornings. Even the birds, motionless in the trees, don't want to whistle and bring it to life. There is a mist out in the distance, rolling from the land to haunt the sea again. This is St Agnes, a village sculptured from rock in Cornwall. I'm in the company of a delightful but eccentric grandmother. She shows me the church hall where Roger Taylor played with his first band, asks me if I'd like to meet the vicar.

And then I'm lost on a dreary housing estate in Leicester, or is it Feltham, hunting for people who will say, "It's such a long time ago" or "I can't remember". I say it doesn't matter, but it does really. I stop and take a photograph of the youth club where John Deacon played his last concert with The Opposition. The nearby bus queue, all hats and anoraks, ponder whether I'm from the council or an estate agents.

I tried to get to everyone, but it was like collecting sand in a sieve. So many people, hidden somewhere in England or France or the United States, or somewhere else. All with a slant, an insight, an anecdote, a memory bleached by time. As I expected, the surviving members of Queen declined to be interviewed, as did their official representatives. "This isn't a cash-in. I want to write all sides," I explained. They'd heard it all before.

Several players in the Queen story are no longer here; many of them Freddie's dearest friends. Others, however, are still with us, pleased to talk. Queen made a lot of friends, at least in the early days, and this book does not deal with what followed their rise to pop eminence. The greed, sexual gratuity, indulgence, boredom, tension and arrogance that might run parallel to extraordinary fame and wealth is someone else's story and they've probably made enough money from it already.

Any biography is only ever a random assembly of thoughts and recollections, held together by analysis and a perfunctory narrative. This is no exception. It already had its 'angle' in its title, so there was no need to resort to scurrility or the inane, or to focus on one band member to the exclusion of the rest.

During the writing of the book I became aware that Queen appeared to have become cool, possibly for the first time ever. New bands namechecked Queen as an influence, some covered their songs. Before Freddie Mercury's death Queen were a critical joke, a pithy abbreviation of comic iconography. Many critics hold the erroneous conviction that death equals respect and Freddie, were he alive, would cackle (not chuckle) at the irony of Queen's new standing.

When Freddie wasted away in his bed at Logan Place, Kensington, even the tabloids which had long salivated over his slow death, wrung genuine words of emotion. The self-assumed sentries of cool, the *NMEs* and *Melody Makers*, took longer of course, several years in fact, but Queen, Freddie, the daft songs, the deft songs, they understood that it all had a point, it meant something.

Queen fulfilled the original rock'n'roll ethos: they never grew up. Sure, they became businessmen with a little too much guile, and much of the clandestine shenanigans were distinctly grown up, but the public persona, the bit we got to see, was a perpetual teenager. Freddie Mercury and his disposable razor songs (his term for them) were the child in us all. When Freddie swaggered, preened, gestured and laughed out loud he was the ten-year-old in the playground, the secret self we should never have lost.